KinderFolders
for Reading Readiness

by Lillian Lieberman
illustrated by Marilynn G. Barr

Publisher: Roberta Suid
Copy Editor: Carol Whiteley
Production: Marilynn G. Barr

For a complete catalog, please write to the address below:
P.O. Box 1680, Palo Alto, CA 94302

ISBN 1-878279-83-1

Printed in the United States of America

987654

TABLE OF CONTENTS

Introduction 4

Letters

1. Turkey Trot (Upper-case letters) 9
2. Snail Trail (Lower-case letters) 13
3. Alphabet Soup (Lower-/upper-case letters) 17
4. Whales Ahoy! (What letter comes before?) 21
5. Happy Hippos (What letter comes in between?) 25
6. Elephant Walk (What letter comes after?) 29
7. Jungle Walk (Upper-case sequence) 33
8. To Grandma's House (Lower-case sequence) 37

Sounds

9. Monkey Business (Initial b, c, f, m) 41
10. Hens and Nests (Initial g, h, n, s) 45
11. Butterfly Wings (Initial d, k, l, w) 49
12. Jumping Beans (Initial j, t, p, z) 53
13. Countdown! (Initial b, c, f, m, g, h, n, s, d, k, l, w, j, t, z, p) ... 57
14. Bugs on a Rug (Final g, n, p, s) 61
15. Three Cubs in a Tub (Final b, f, m, x) 65
16. Bats in Hats (Final d, l, r, t) 69
17. Caterpillar (Final r, b, d, f, g, l, m, n, p, s, t, x) 73
18. Alligator's Party (Short vowels a, i, o) 77
19. Ducks in the Pond (Short vowels u, e) 81
20. The Beetle Band (All short vowels) 85
21. Piggy's Ice Cream Sodas (Rhyming picture match) 89

Sounds

22. Mouse Party (Initial p, c, f, z, t, y, j) 93
23. Net the Fish! (Initial g, n, s, k, r, b, v) 97
24. Ants on a Hill (Initial q, l, h, d, m, w) 101
25. Foxes in Boxes (Final b, f, m, r, t, x) 105
26. Bus Station (Final d, g, l, n, p, s) 109
27. Otters and Shells (Initial a, e, i, o, u) 113
28. Frogs on a Log (Medial a, e, i, o, u) 117

Words

29. Dinosaur Rhymes (Rhyming word families) 121
30. Color Wagon (Color words) 125
31. Merry-go-round (Reading short vowel words) 129
32. Number Wheel (Number words, one to ten) 133
33. Sight Word Dive (Beginning sight words) 137
34. Make a Rainbow (Phrase reading and sentences) 141

Introduction

KinderFolders for Reading Readiness presents activities to enrich reading readiness skills for preschoolers, kindergartners, and first graders in easy-to-make-and-use file folder set-ups. The folders can be used with individual children, small cooperative groups, or in learning centers.

The activities in *KinderFolders for Reading Readiness* help to reinforce pre-reading and beginning-reading learning in an enjoyable format. The activities range from alphabet identification to beginning reading of phonetic words. In order to develop reading readiness skills, children do such work as match upper-case letters on clothespin turkey feathers, find the missing letters on elephants, put matching-picture caps on monkeys, and put matching-sound T-shirts on the animals at Alligator's party. Children will also enjoy the challenge of reading simple words on a merry-go-round and matching sight words on a sight-word dive. A variety of hands-on responses, including placing objects, clipping on clothespins, and turning a spinner, keep the children actively engaged.

Titles of related books are included to make the literature connection. These books may be used to help initiate the activities as well as to enhance the children's enjoyment and involvement in learning. The books should be read to the children and made available for their use.

Each *KinderFolder* activity includes the file folder layout and the activity to be duplicated, simple directions for use, and a suggested book to read. A tab label and an illustration for the folder cover are also provided. Place the directions below the cover illustration to facilitate use. General construction and use directions follow here. The "How to Make Instant Folders" section provides additional information for particular activities.

General Directions

Construction

Use sturdy colored file folders for the *KinderFolder* folders. Duplicate the inside file folder set-up, the illustration for the activity, and the activity label. Color with felt pens, colored pencils, or crayons. Then trim and cut out. Glue the file folder set-up to the inside of the folder and the illustration to the outside front. Glue the directions with the "Book to Read" reference below the illustration. Glue the tab label onto the file folder tab. Laminate both sides of the file folder.

Glue the duplicated sheets, along with any loose parts, such as markers or spinners, onto oak tag for sturdiness. Color and laminate. Cut out or trim as necessary and complete construction. A craft knife is recommended for making the slits and slots for the activities that require them. Buttons or other objects can be used for markers that are not provided. Glue a 7 1/2" x 10 1/2" manila clasp envelope to the back of the file folder to hold loose parts.

Activity Use

Have the children take out any loose parts from the envelope and open the file folder on the work area. Instruct the children on how to play, referring to the directions. Have the children replace the parts in the envelope after play and deposit the folder in a file basket. If possible, read the recommended book prior to each activity for added motivation.

How to Make Instant Folders

Match-ups and Game Boards
(Activities 7-14, 17-29, 33-34)

Follow the general directions. For "Jungle Walk" and "To Grandma's House," provide die and markers. Duplicate extra activity sheets. Glue to oak tag, color, and laminate. Enclose in a manila envelope with a washable pen or erasable crayon.

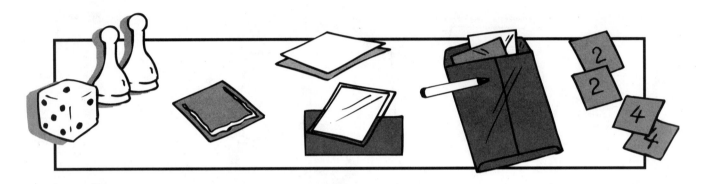

Clothespin Matches
(Activities 1-6)

Follow the general directions. Cut out and glue the labels securely to the clothespins. Reinforce with clear sealing tape if desired. Cut out the parts for the file folder set-up. Laminate and glue onto the file folder. Leave free of glue the areas where clothespins will be attached. Cut out the extra activities. Color and laminate. Place in the envelope. For "Alphabet Soup" and "Snail Trail," place a washable felt pen or erasable crayon in the envelope.

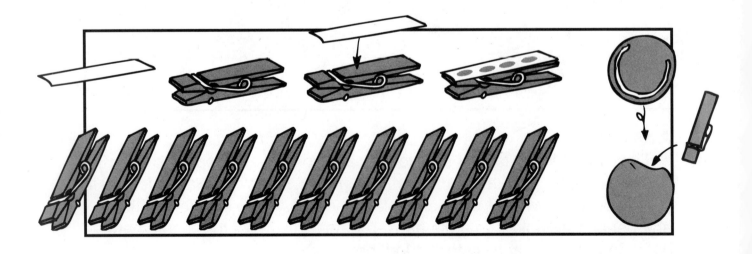

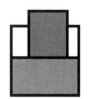

Slip-ins
(Activities 15-16)

Follow the general directions. For "Three Cubs in a Tub," make a slit on the dotted lines on the tub with a craft knife. Spread glue on the outer edge on the back of the tubs, leaving the area around the slit free of glue. Secure to the folder. Do the same for the hats in "Bats in Hat." Glue the sheets of loose parts to oak tag. Color, laminate, and cut out. Place in a manila envelope.

Spinner Set-ups
(Activities 30-32)

Follow the general directions. Duplicate parts for the spinner and wheel. Color and glue to oak tag. Laminate and cut out. Punch a hole in the center of the wheel with a sharp tool and attach the spinner with a brass fastener. Provide buttons or other objects for markers and place in a Ziplock™ plastic bag. Place the wheel and the markers in a manila envelope.

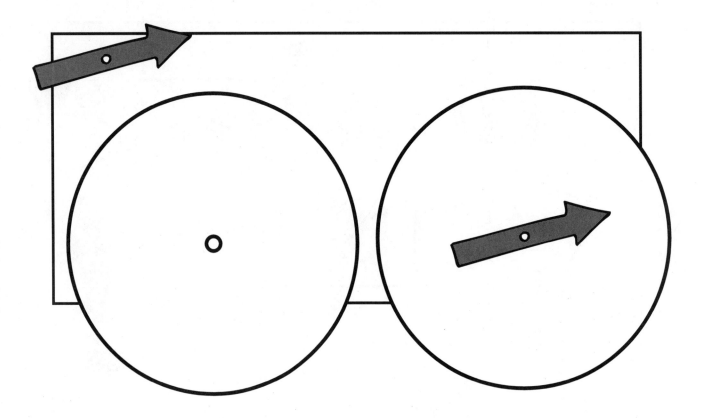

1. Turkey Trot

Turkey Trot

Upper-case letters

Directions: Take out the clothespin letter feathers and open the folder. Name the upper-case letters on the feathers. Match each letter to the same letter on a turkey. Clip the clothespin to the letter.

A book to read: Sometimes It's Turkey, Sometimes It's Feathers by Lorna Balian

Turkey Trot

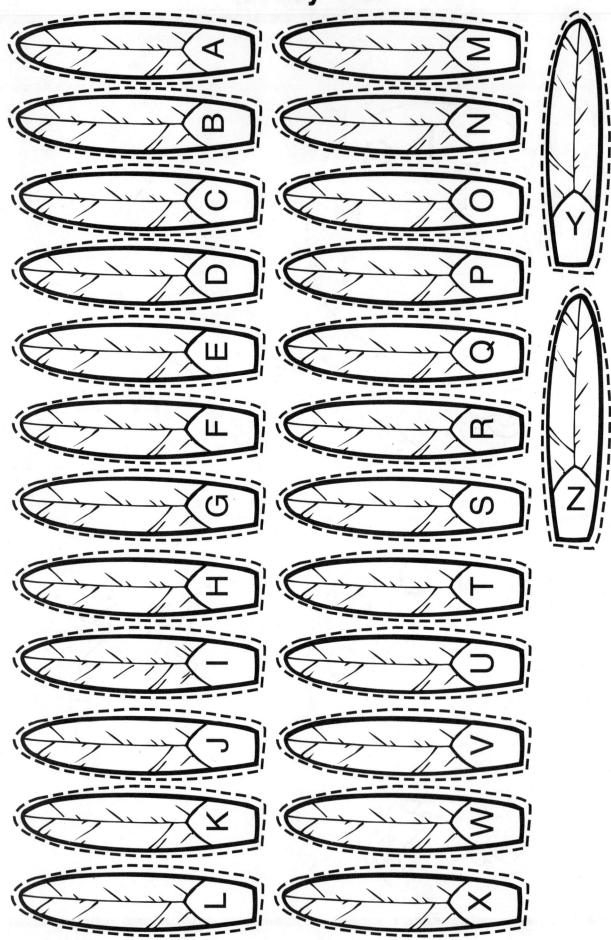

12

Snail Trail

Activity Card

Snail Trail

Lower-case letters

Directions: Take out the clothespin letters and open the folder. Name the lower-case letters on the clothespins. Find the matching letters on the snails. Clip each clothespin letter to the matching letter on a snail. For the activity card, use the washable felt pen or erasable crayon to connect the dots in order from a to z.

A book to read: Snail Spell by Joanna Ryder

Snail Trail

14

Snail Trail

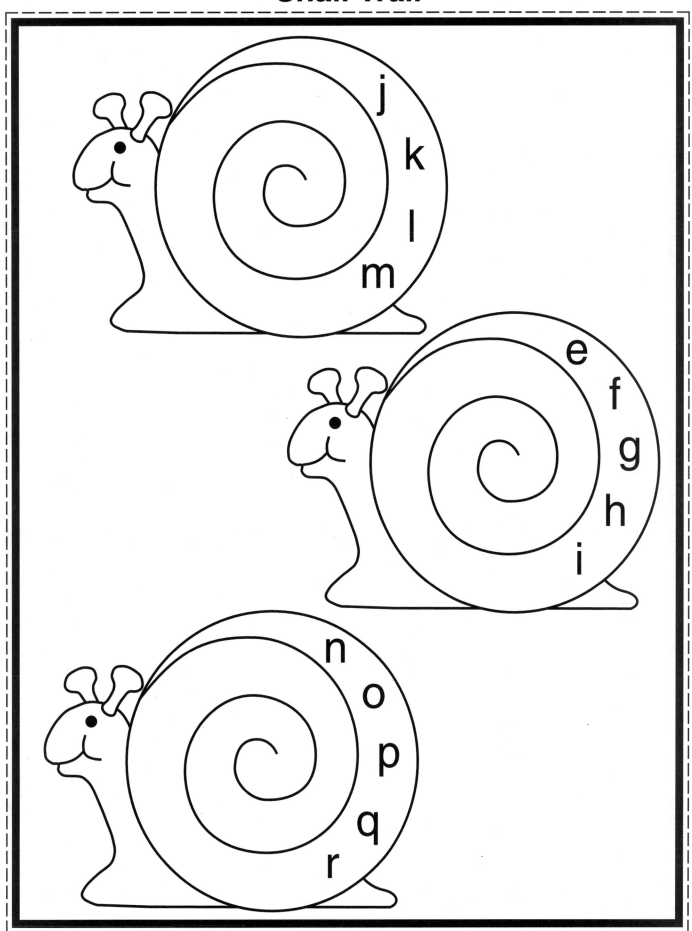

15

Snail Trail

Clothespin Letters

a b c d e f g h i j k l

m n o p q r s t u v w x

y z

Activity Card

c. d.
b. e.
a. f.
t.
s. u. g.
r.
z. v. h.
q. y.
p. i.
x. w.
o. j.
n. k.
m. l.

Alphabet Soup

Lower-/upper-case letters

Directions: Take out the clothespin upper-case letters and open the folder. Name the upper-case letters. Find the matching lower-case letters in the alphabet soup bowls. Clip each clothespin letter to the matching letter on a bowl. For the activity card, use the pen or crayon to draw a line between matching upper-case and lower-case letters.

A book to read: Alpha Beta Chowder by Jeanne and Willam Steig

Alphabet Soup

Alphabet Soup

Alphabet Soup

A	B	C	D	E	F	G	H	I	J	K	L
M	N	O	P	Q	R	S	T	U	V	W	X
Y	Z										

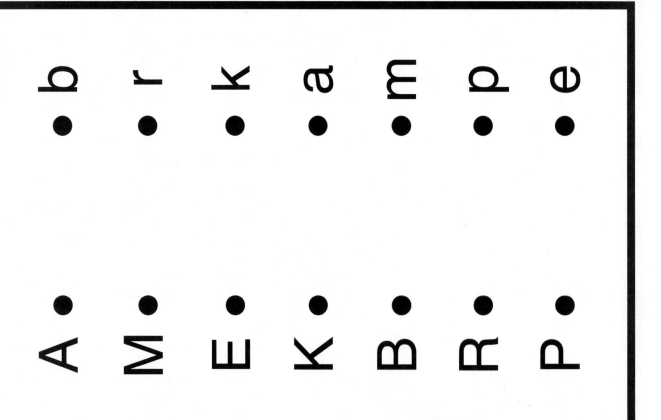

Whales Ahoy!

Whales Ahoy!

What letter comes before?

Directions: Take out the clothespin letters and open the folder. Name the letters. Find the missing letter that comes before on each whale. Clip the letter to the whale. Take out the little whales. Line them up in abc order. Say all the letters in order.

A book to read: Winter Whale by Joanna Ryder

Whales Ahoy!

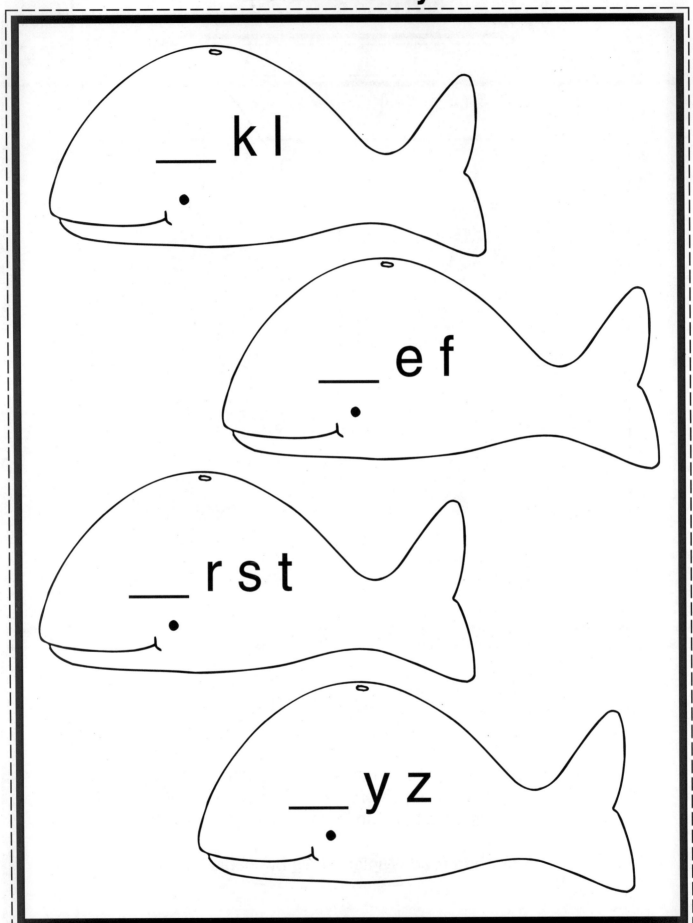

_ k l

_ e f

_ r s t

_ y z

© 1995 Monday Morning Books, Inc.

22

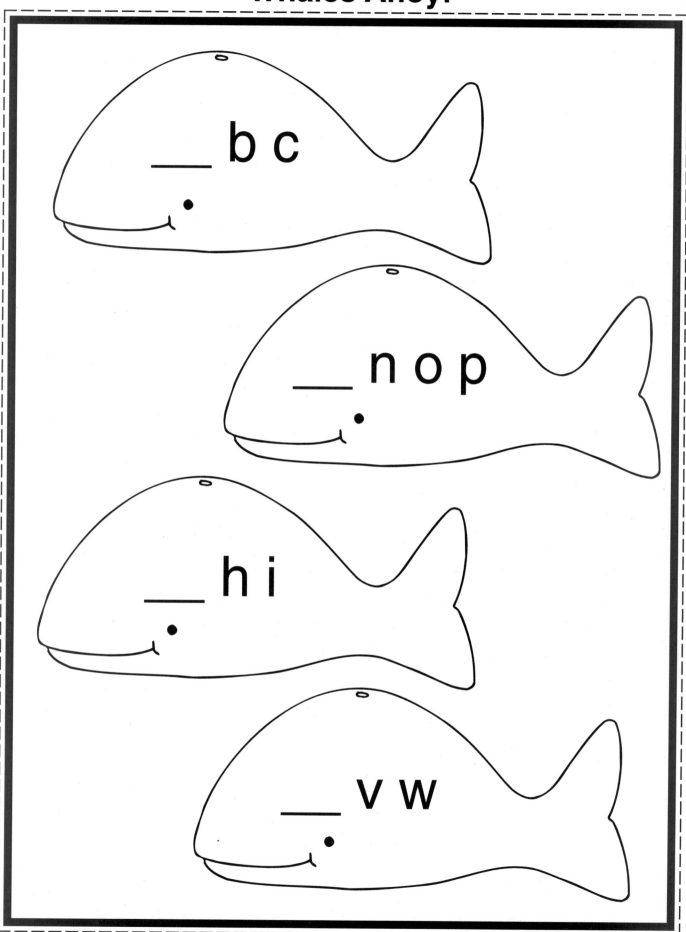

Whales Ahoy!

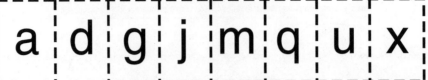

a d g j m q u x

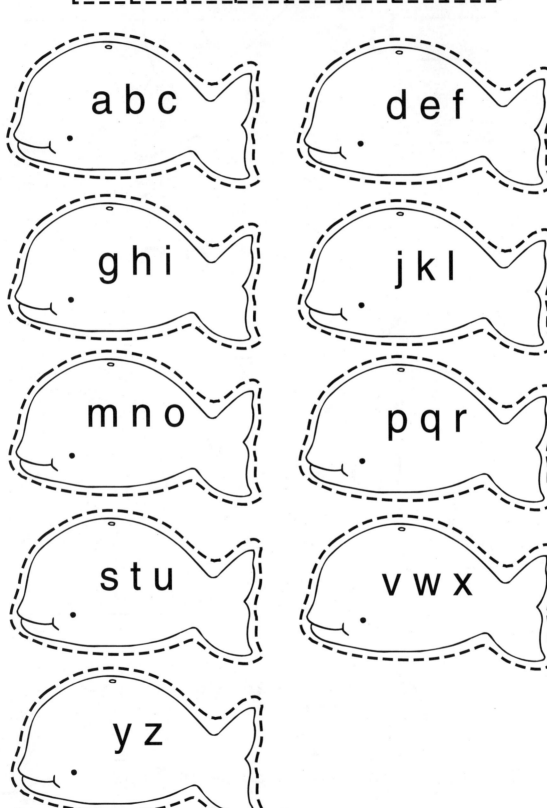

a b c

d e f

g h i

j k l

m n o

p q r

s t u

v w x

y z

24

Happy Hippos

What letter comes in between?

Directions: Take out the clothespin letters and open the folder. Name the letters. Find the missing letter that comes in between on each hippo. Clip the missing letter on the hippo. Take out the little hippos. Line them up in ABC order. Say all the letters in order.

A book to read: <u>Hippo Lemonade</u> by Mike Thaler

Happy Hippos

a __ c

m __ o

g __ i

t u __ w

j __ l

p __ r s

d __ f

x __ z

Happy Hippos

b e h k n q v y

ABC

DEF

GHI

JKL

MNO

PQR

STU

VWX

YZ

Elephant Walk

What letter comes after?

Directions: Take out the clothespin letters and open the folder. Name the letters. Find the missing letter that comes after on each elephant. Clip the letter to each elephant. Take out the little elephants. Line them up in abc order. Say all the letters in order.

A book to read: <u>Allistairs Elephant</u> by Marilyn Sadler

Elephant Walk

a b __

n o __

d e __

t u __

30

Elephant Walk

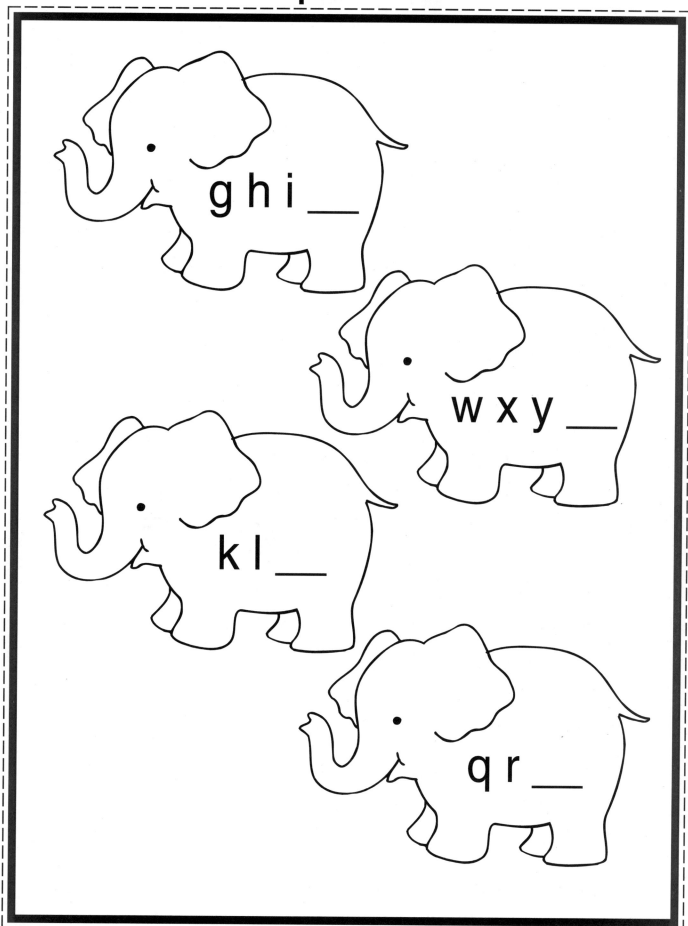

g h i __

w x y __

k l __

q r __

31

Elephant Walk

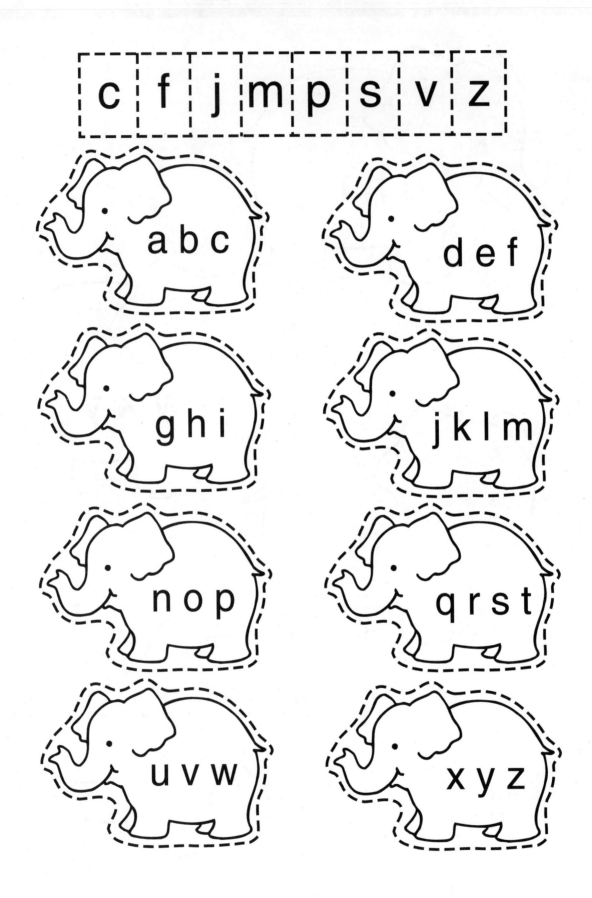

| c | f | j | m | p | s | v | z |

a b c

d e f

g h i

j k l m

n o p

q r s t

u v w

x y z

32

7

Jungle Walk

Jungle Walk

Upper-case sequence

Directions: Two children may play. Take out the die and the markers. Open the folder. Throw the die in turn. Move your marker the number of spaces the die shows. Name the upper-case letters as you move. To complete the walk, you must roll the exact number that lets you land on Stop. The first one to reach Stop is the winner. For the activity cards, use the pen or crayon to connect the dots in ABC order.

A book to read: <u>Walking Through the Jungle</u> by Julie Lacome

Jungle Walk

34

Jungle Walk

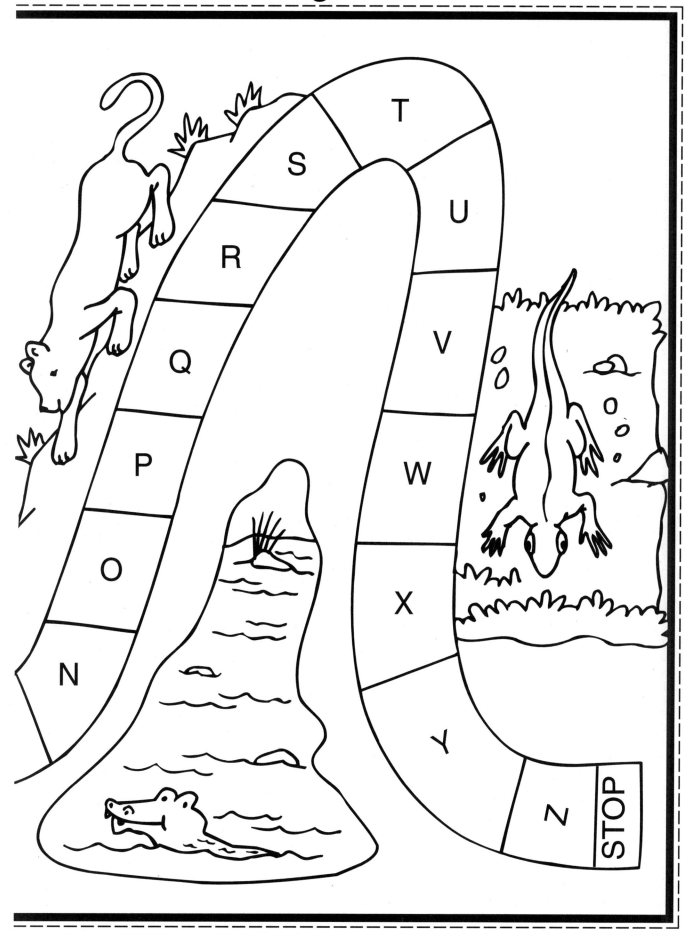

35

Jungle Walk

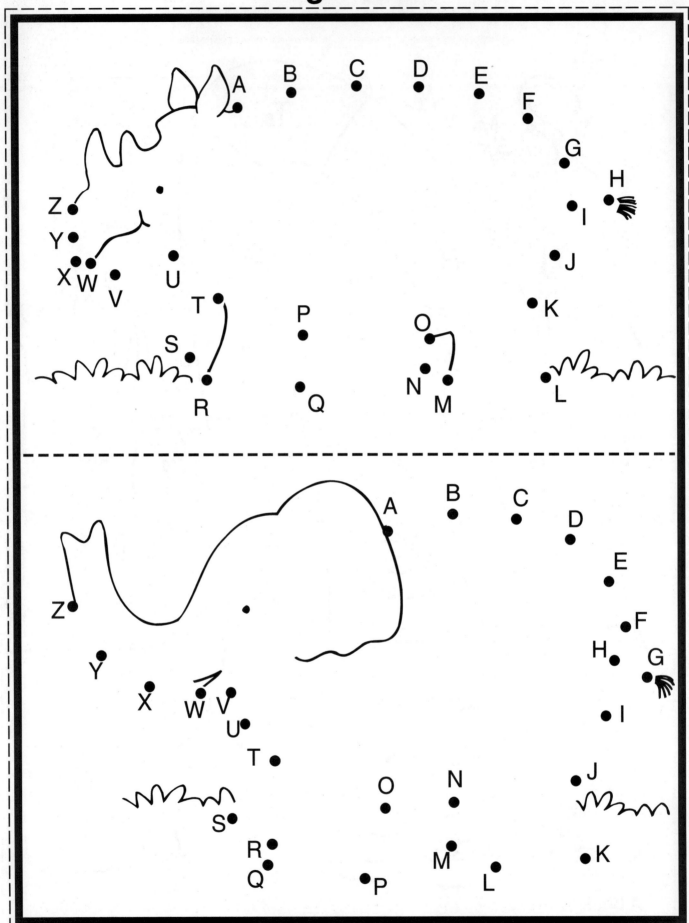

8

To Grandma's House

To Grandma's House

Lower-case sequence

Directions: Two children may play. Take out the die and the markers. Open the folder. Pick a marker. Throw the die in turn. Move your marker the number of spaces the die shows. Name the lower-case letters as you move. To complete the walk, you must roll the exact number that lets you land on Stop. The first one to reach Stop gets to Grandma's birthday party first! For the activity cards, use the pen or crayon to connect the dots in abc order.

A book to read: <u>A Secret for Grandmother's Birthday</u> by Franz Brandenburg

To Grandma's House

Go a b c d e f g

r q p o

s

t

u v w x y

To Grandma's House

39

To Grandma's House

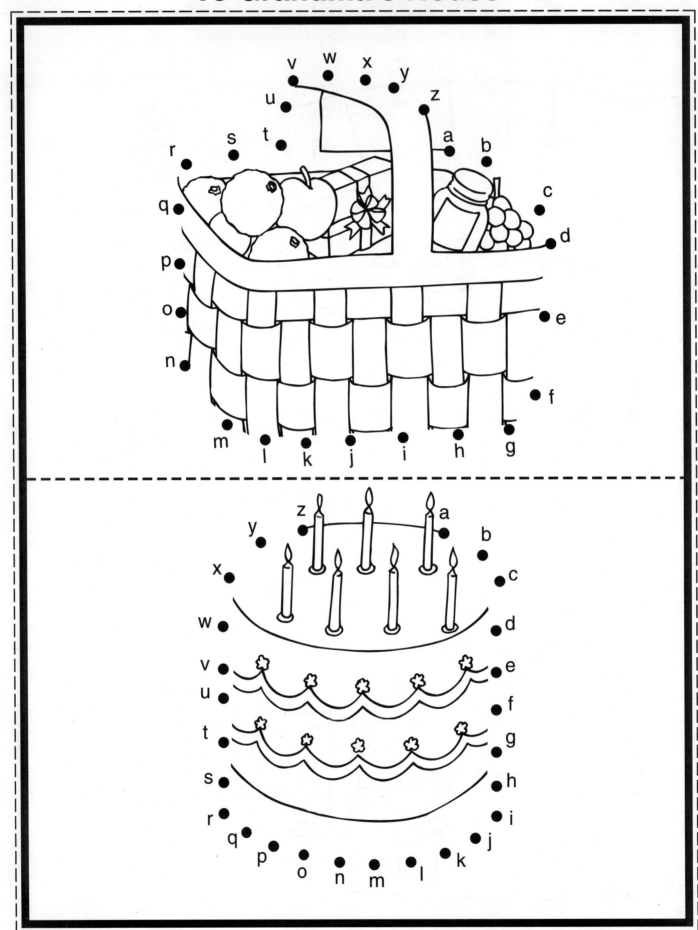

40

9

Monkey Business

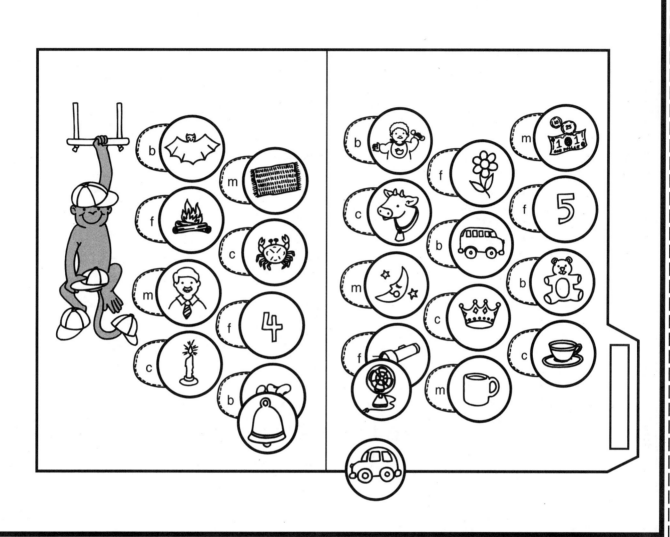

Monkey Business

Initial b, c, f, m

Directions: Take out the circles and open the folder. Name the picture on each circle. Find the picture that has the same beginning sound as a cap circle on the folder. Put it on the cap. Find the matching cap for each circle.

A book to read: <u>Caps for Sale</u> by Esphyr Slobodkina

Monkey Business

42

Monkey Business

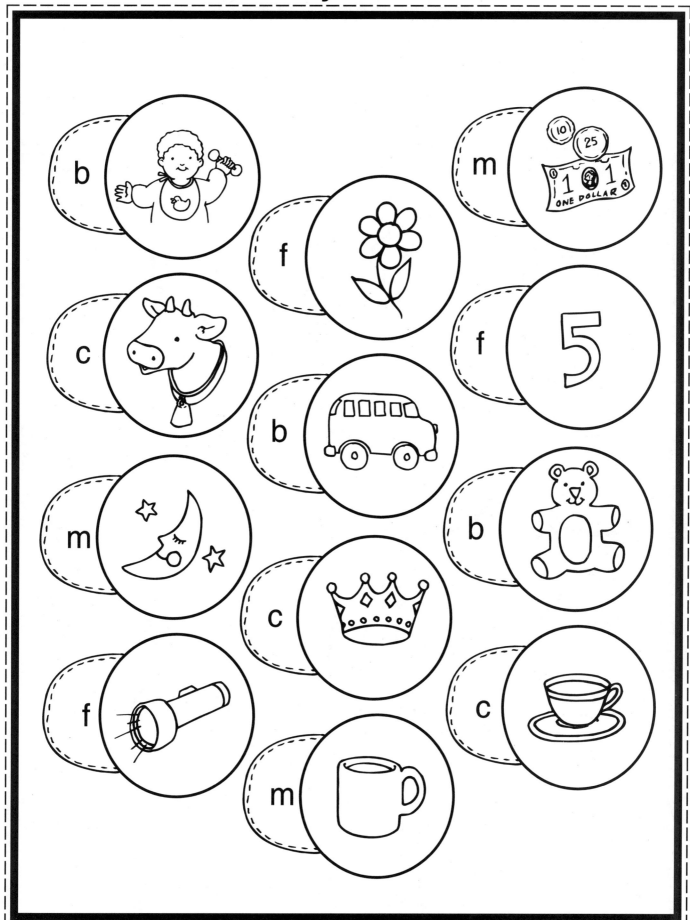

43

Monkey Business

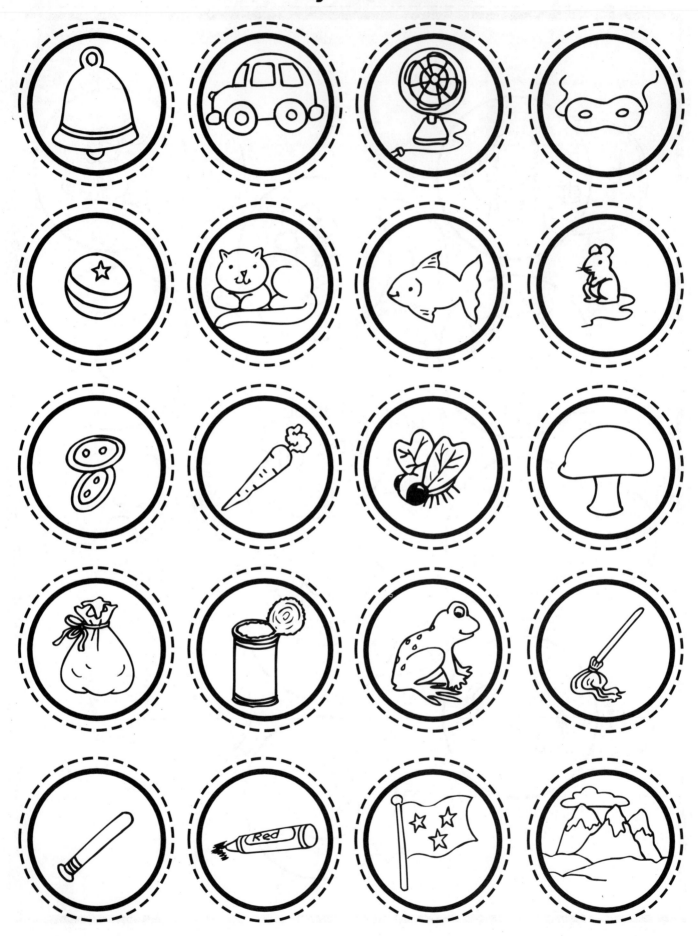

44

10. Hens and Nests

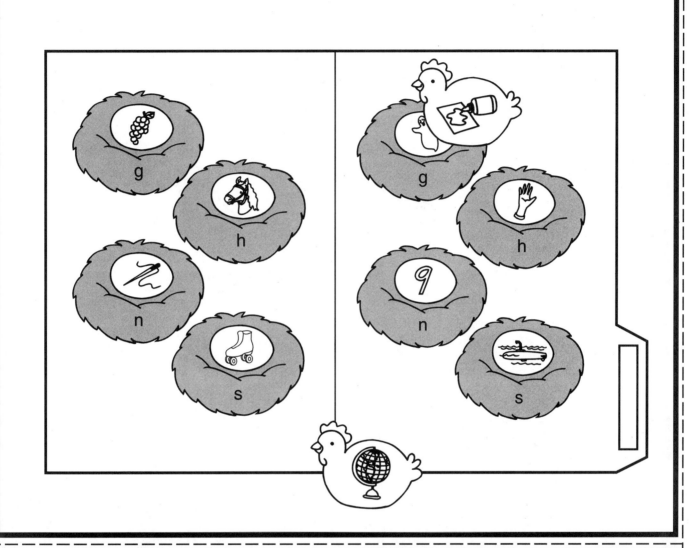

Hens and Nests

Initial g, h, n, s

Directions: Take out the hens and open the folder. Name the pictures on the hens. Find the picture that has the same beginning sound as a picture on a nest. Put the right hen on each nest.

A book to read: Big Fat Hen by Keith Baker

Hens and Nests

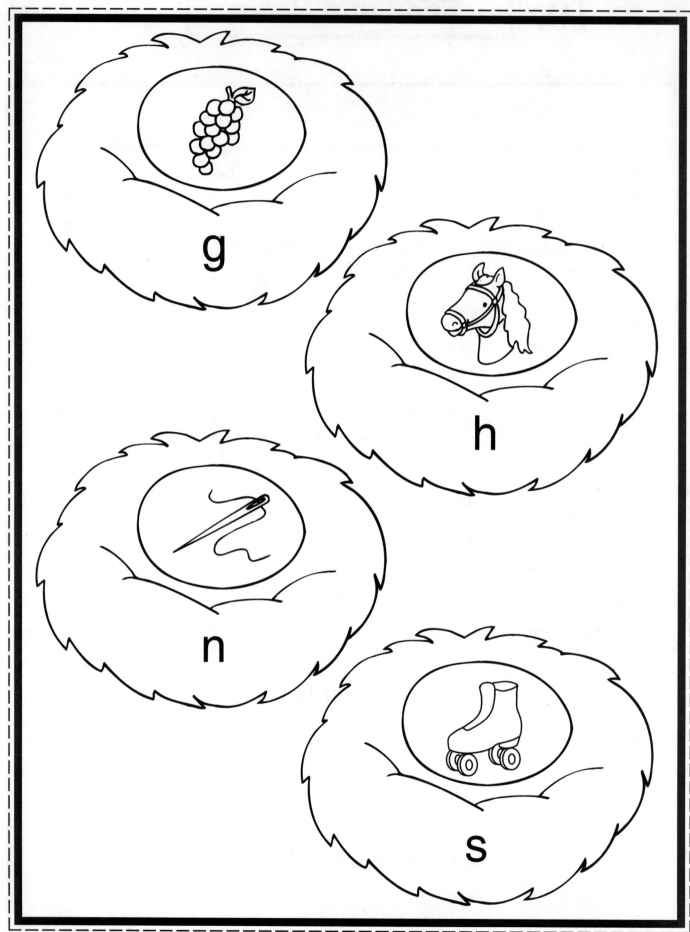

g

h

n

s

Hens and Nests

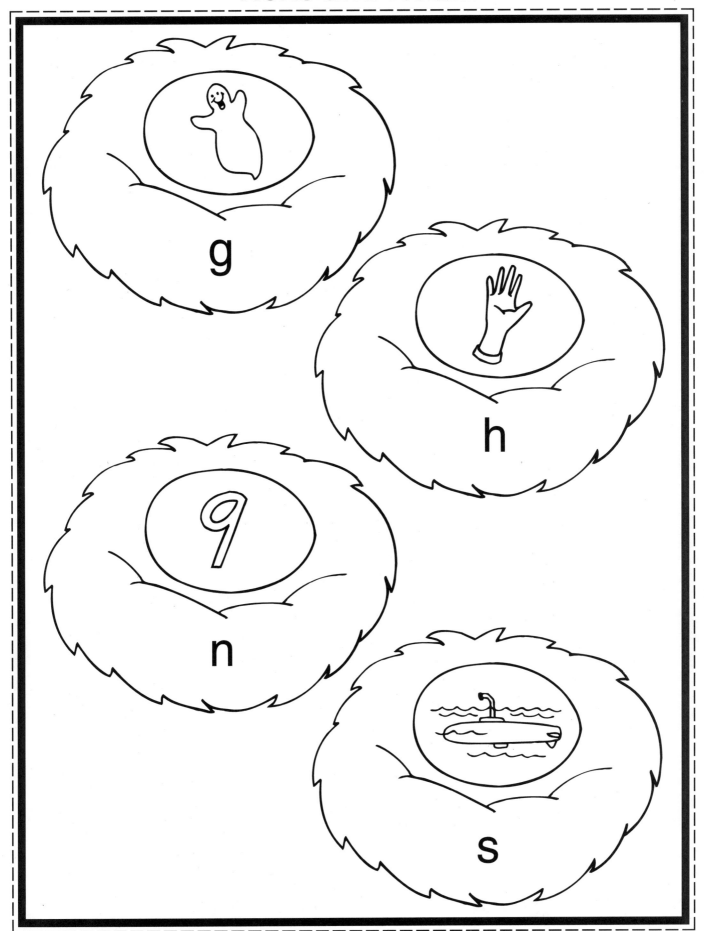

Hens and Nests

48

Butterfly Wings

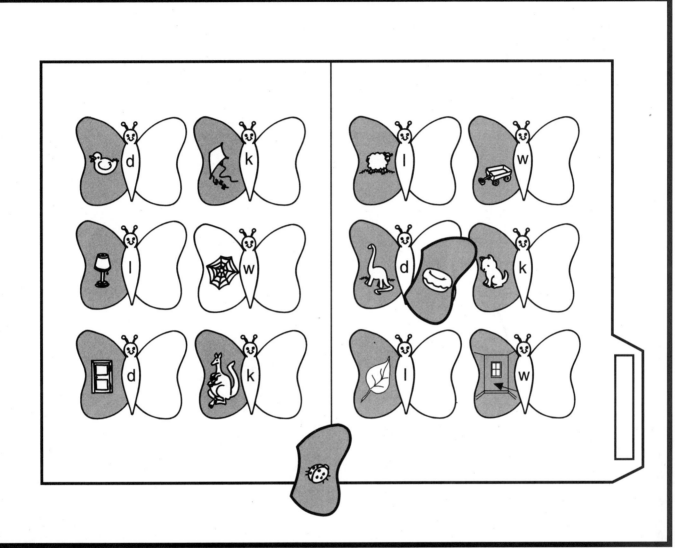

Butterfly Wings

Initial d, k, l, w

Directions: Take out the butterfly wings and open the folder. Name the pictures on the wings. Find the wing that has the same beginning sound as the picture on a butterfly. Put the right wing on each butterfly.

A book to read: <u>Where Butterflies Grow</u> by Joanna Ryder

Butterfly Wings

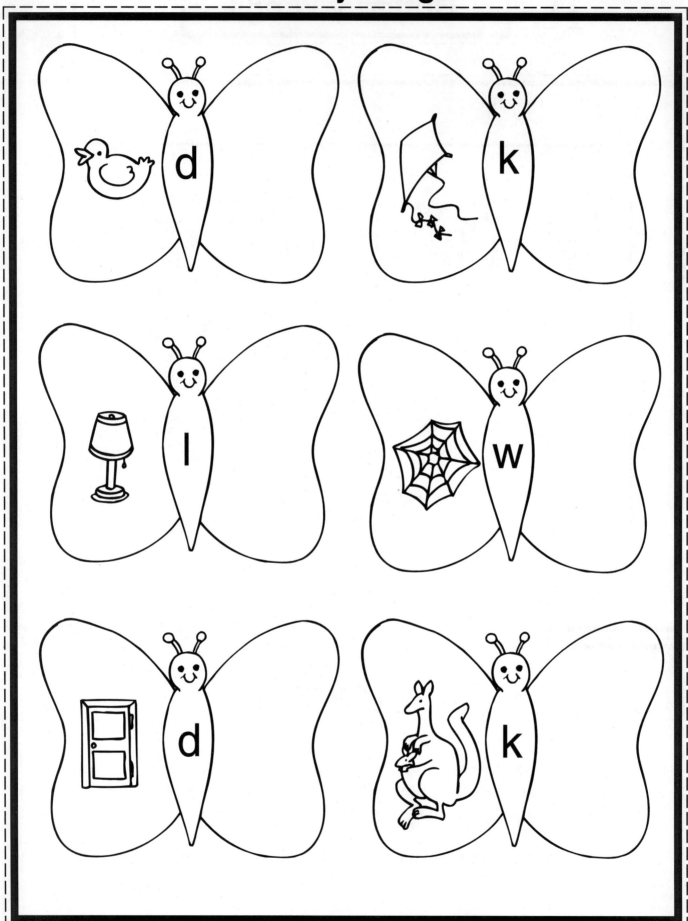

Butterfly Wings

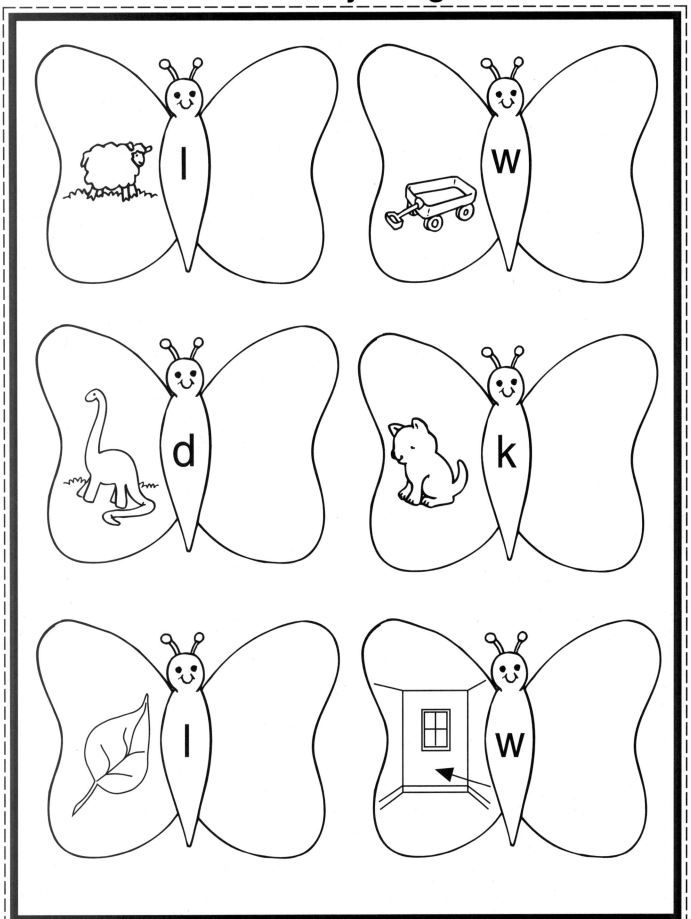

Butterfly Wings

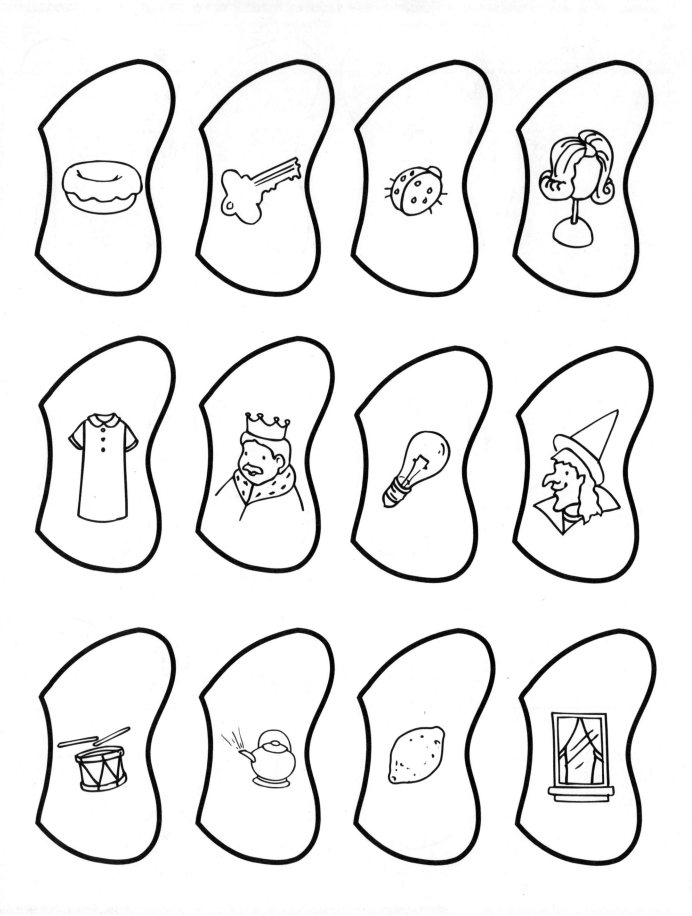

Jumping Beans

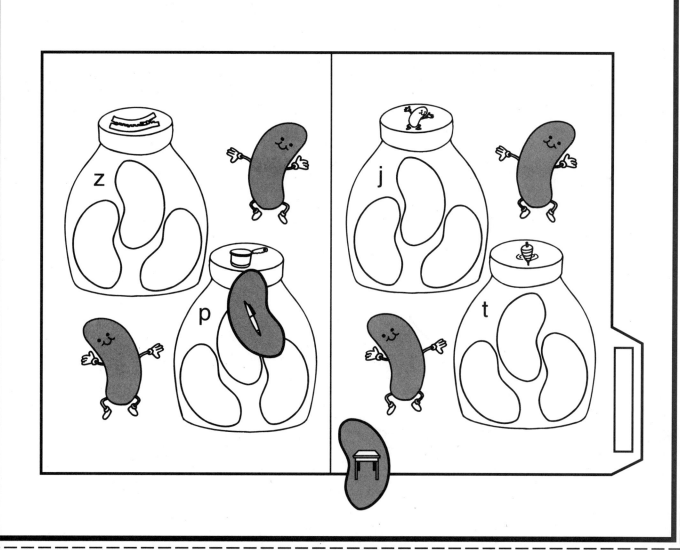

Jumping Beans

Initial j, t, p, z

Directions: Take out the beans and open the folder. Name the pictures on the beans. Find the jar that has a picture with the same beginning sound as the picture on each bean. Put the right beans on each jar.

A book to read: <u>Jumping Beans</u> by Edna Miller

Jumping Beans

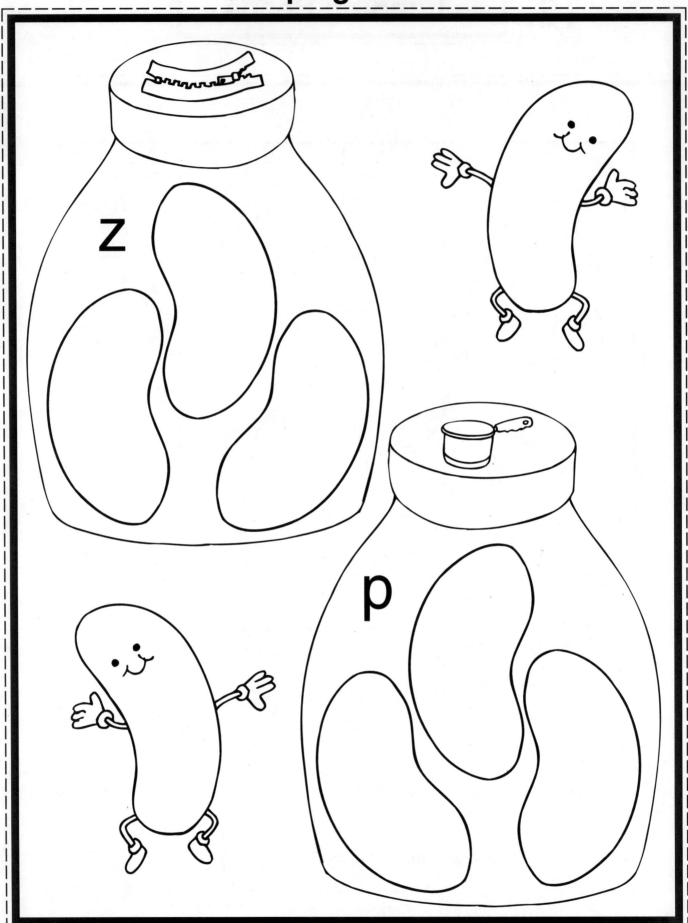

54

Jumping Beans

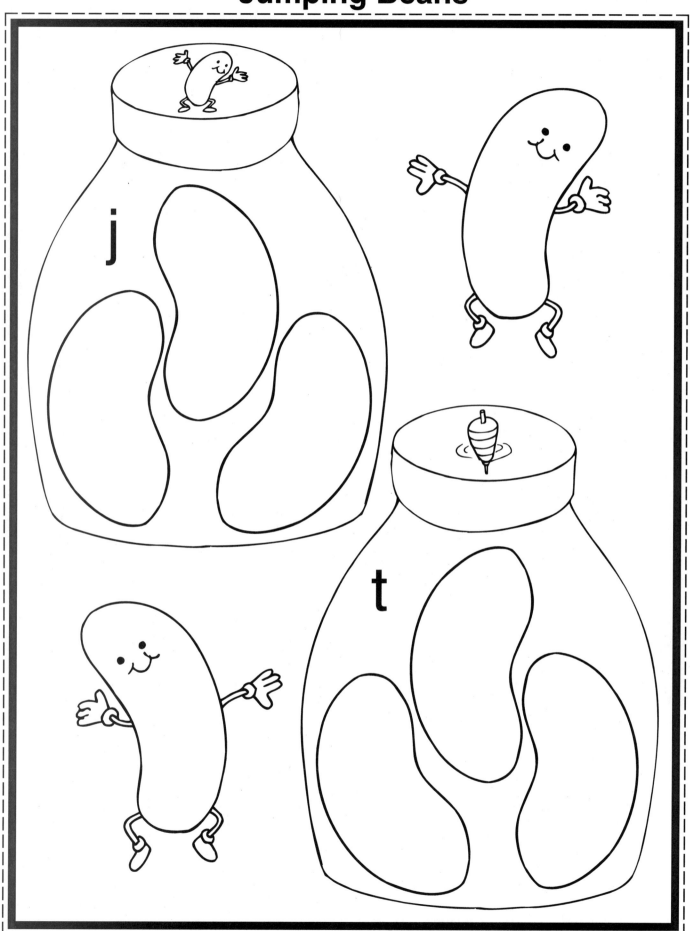

Jumping Beans

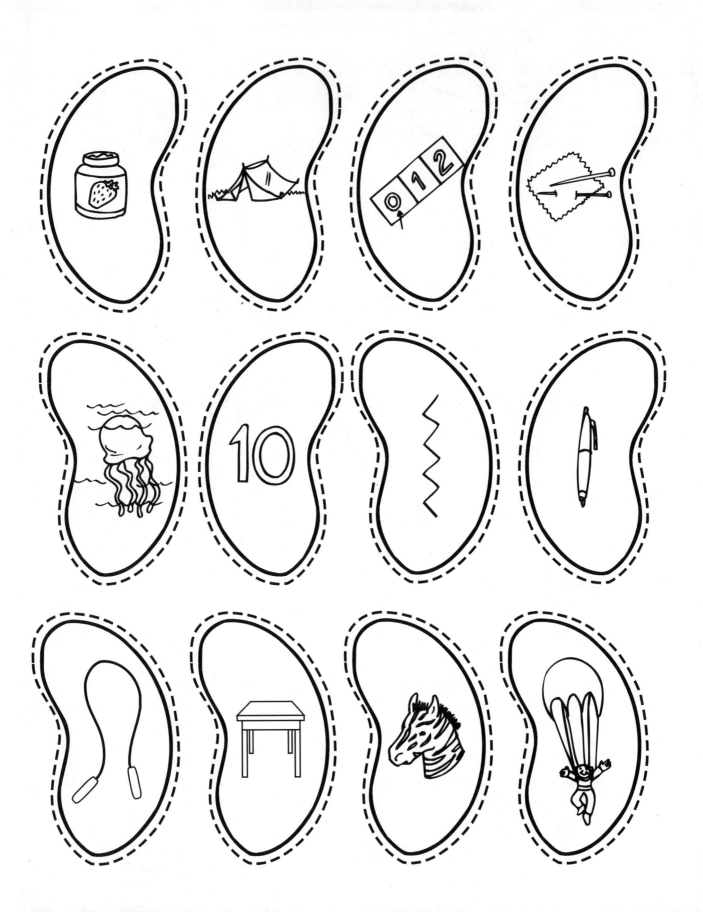

13. | Countdown!

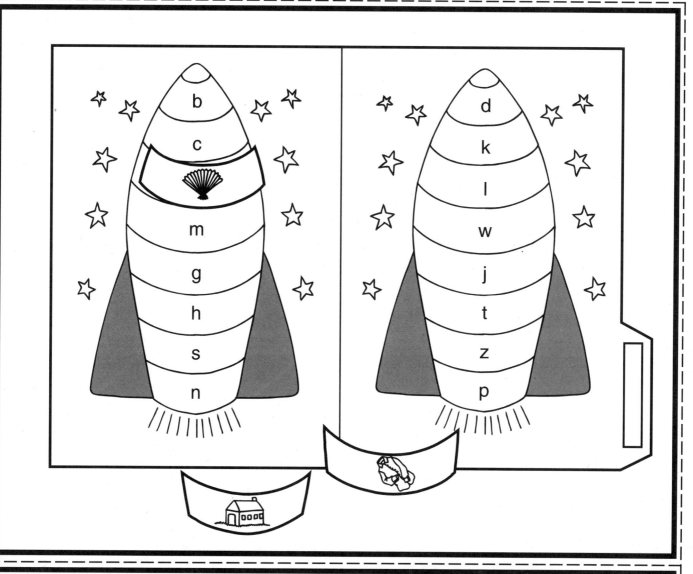

Countdown!

Initial b, c, f, m, g, h, n, s, d, k, l, w, j, t, z, p

Directions: Take out the rocket parts and open the folder. Name the pictures on the parts. Find the rocket part that has a picture with the same beginning sound as a letter on the rocket. Put each matching part on the rocket.

A book to read: <u>Going to the Moon</u> by James Muirden

Countdown!

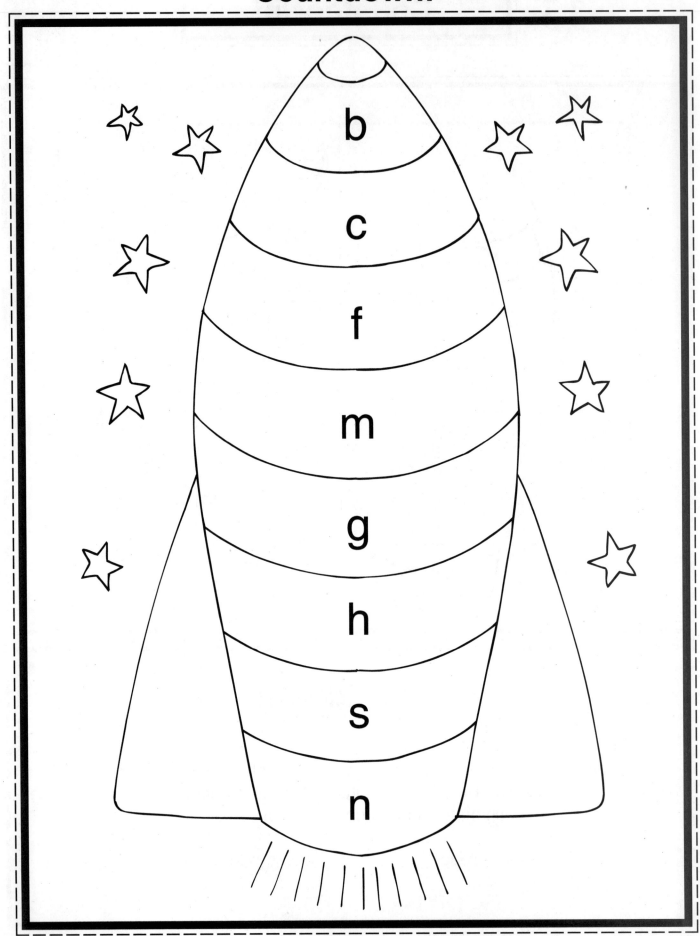

58

Countdown!

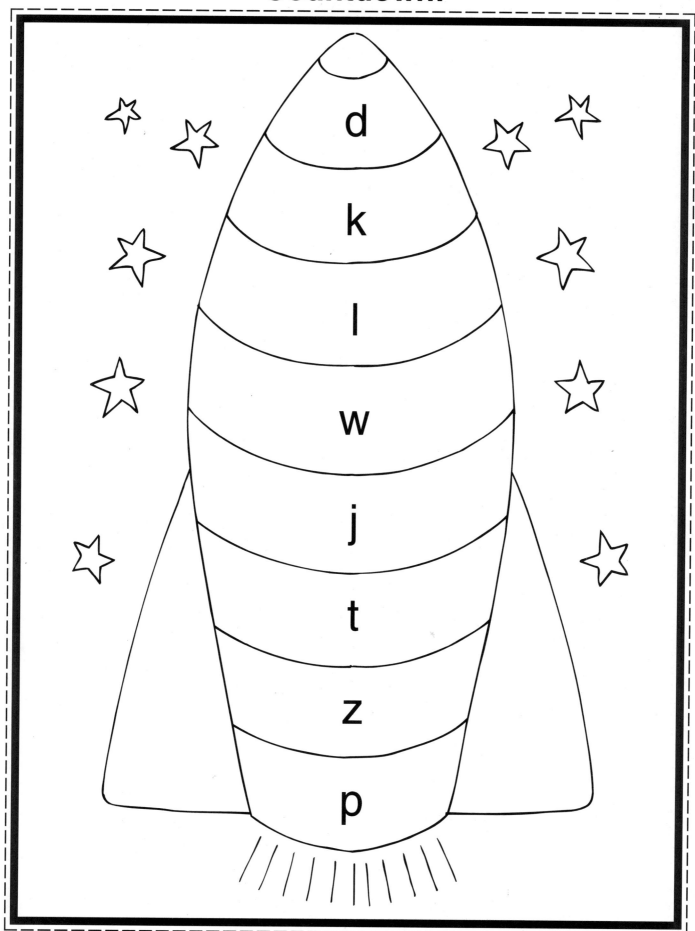

Countdown!

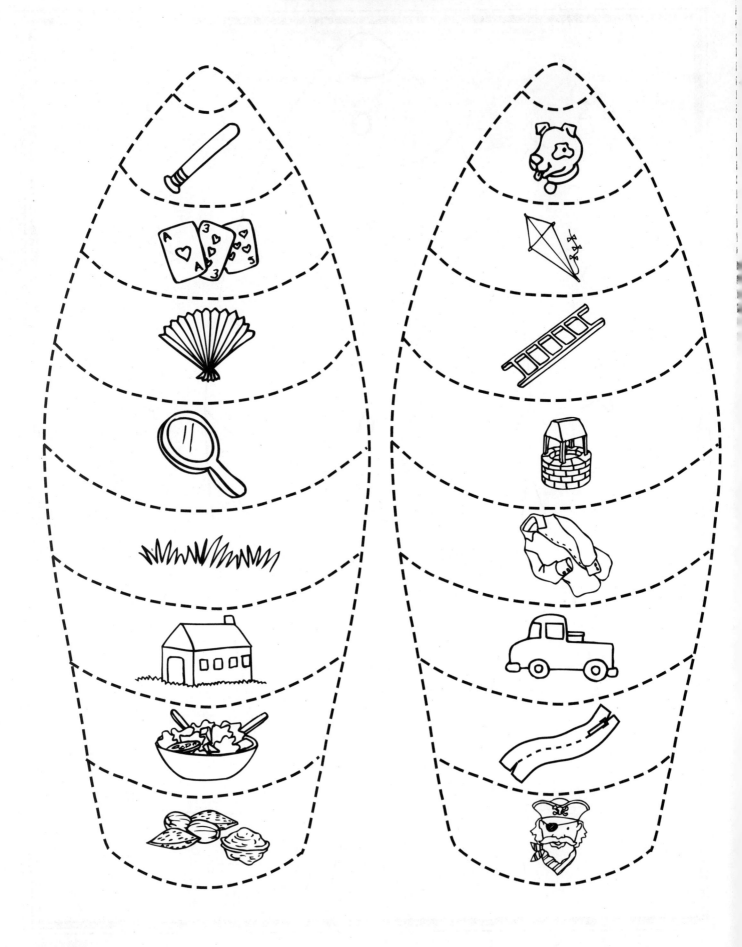

60

Bugs on a Rug

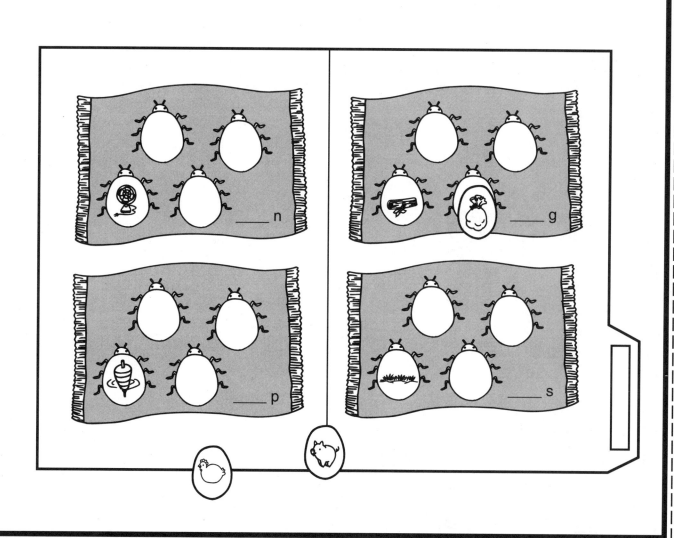

Bugs on a Rug

Final g, n, p, s

Directions: Take out the circles and open the folder. Name the pictures on the circles. Find the bug on the rug that has the same ending sound as each picture circle. Put the right circle on each bug on the rug.

A book to read: <u>Because a Little Bug Went Ka-Choo</u> by Rosetta Stone

Bugs on a Rug

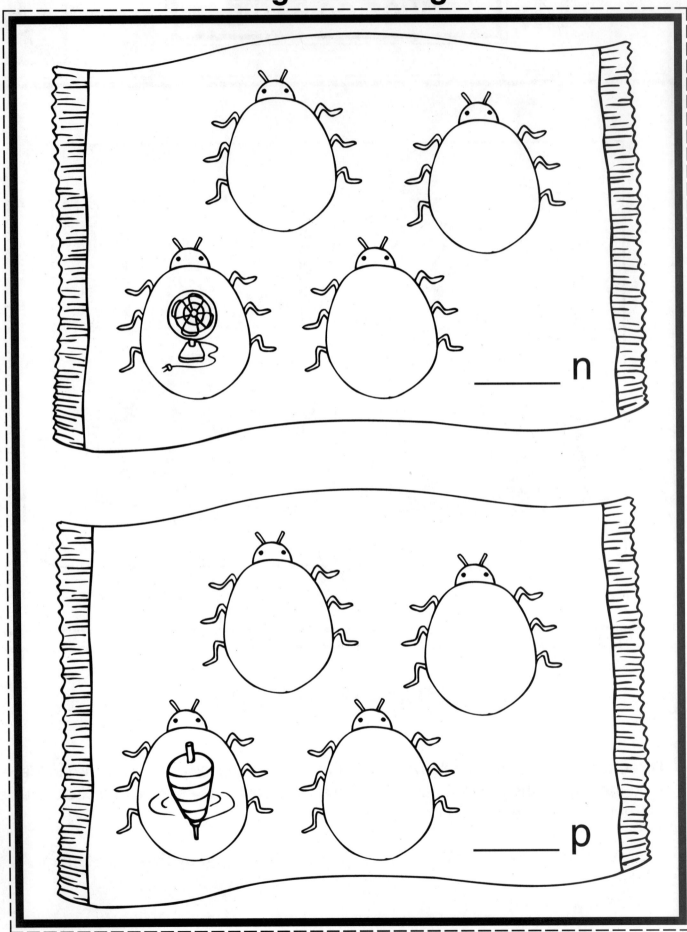

_____ n

_____ p

Bugs on a Rug

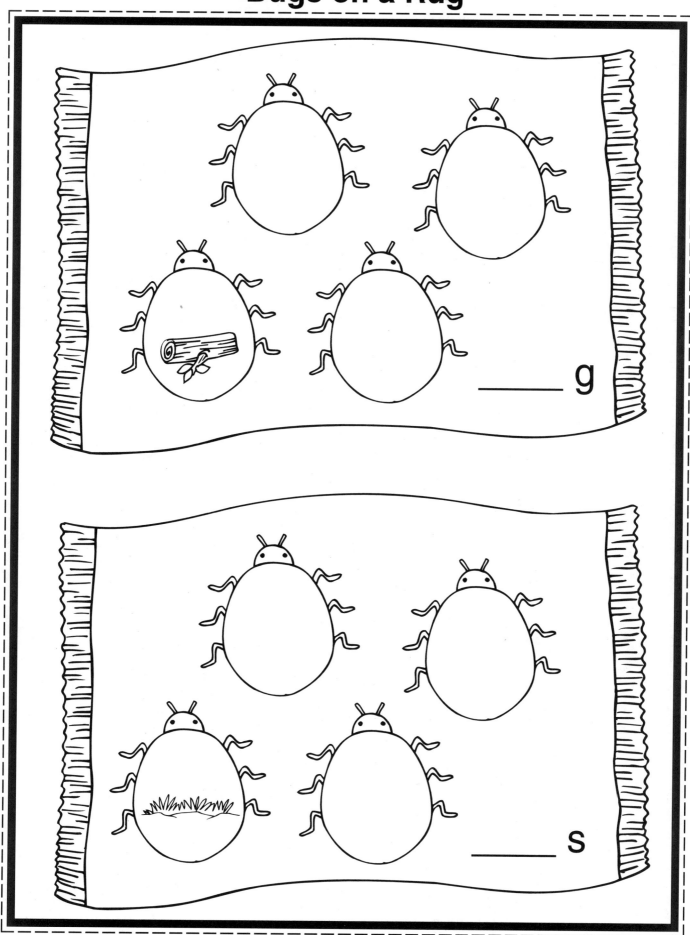

_____ g

_____ s

Bugs on a Rug

64

15. | Three Cubs in a Tub

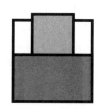

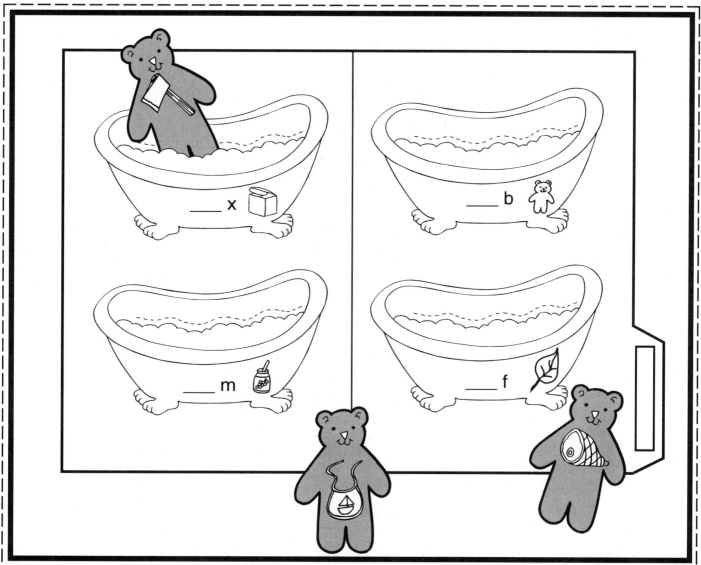

Three Cubs in a Tub

Final b, f, m, x

Directions: Take out the cubs and open the folder. Name the pictures on the cubs. Find the tub that has a picture with the same ending sound as the picture on each cub. Slip the right cubs into each tub.

A book to read: Two Bear Cubs by Anna Jonas

Three Cubs in a Tub

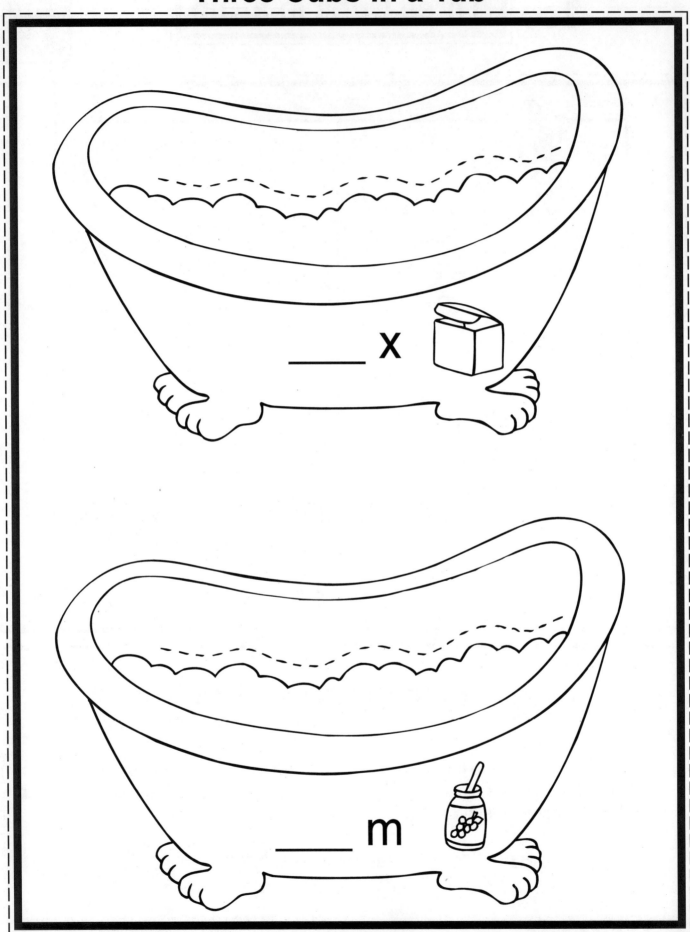

_____ x

_____ m

Three Cubs in a Tub

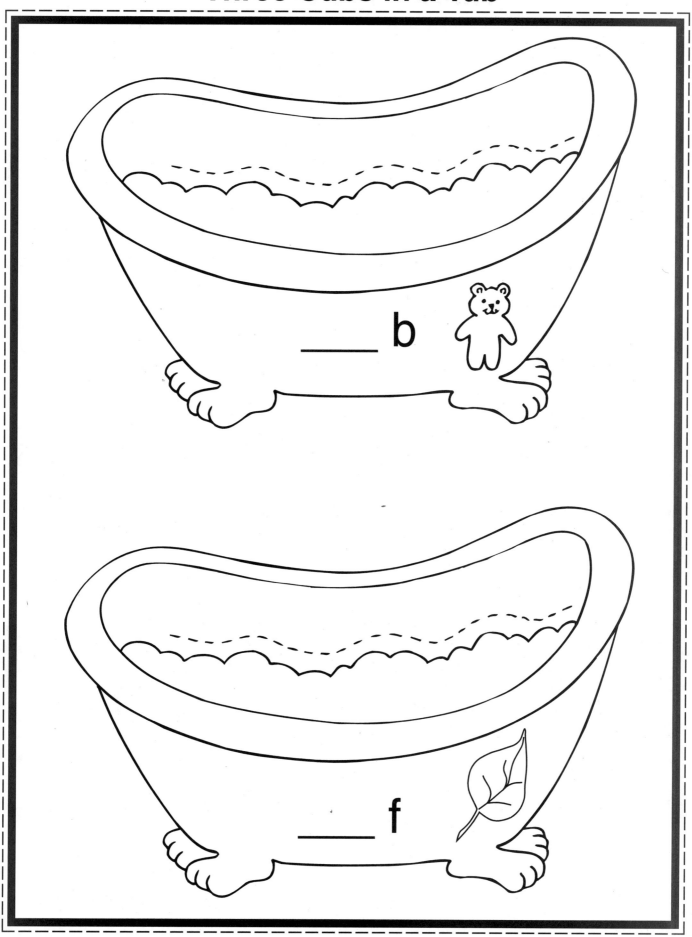

___ b

___ f

Three Cubs in a Tub

16

Bats in Hats

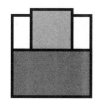

Bats in Hats

Final d, l, r, t

Directions: Take out the bats and open the folder. Name the picture on each bat. Find the hat whose picture has the same ending sound. Slip the matching bats into each hat.

A book to read: <u>Stellaluna</u> by Jannel Cannon

Bats in Hats

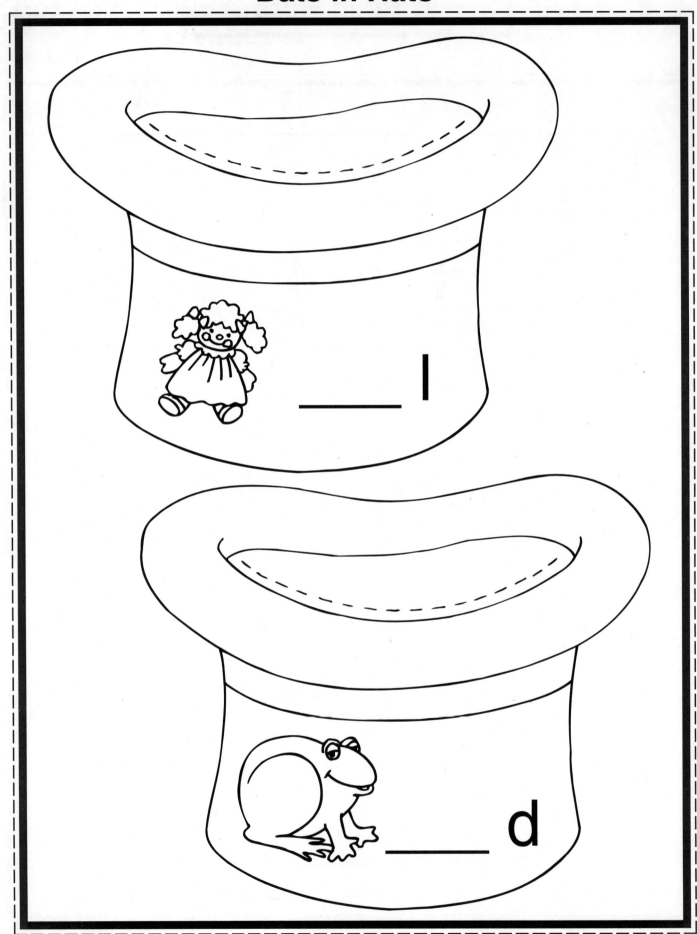

_____ l

_____ d

Bats in Hats

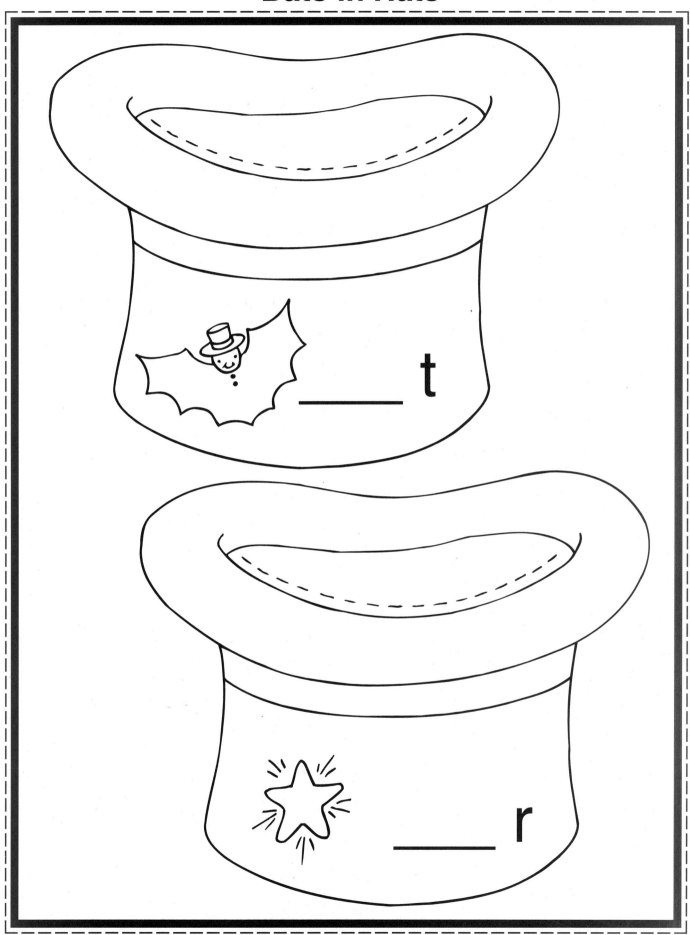

___t

___r

Bats in Hats

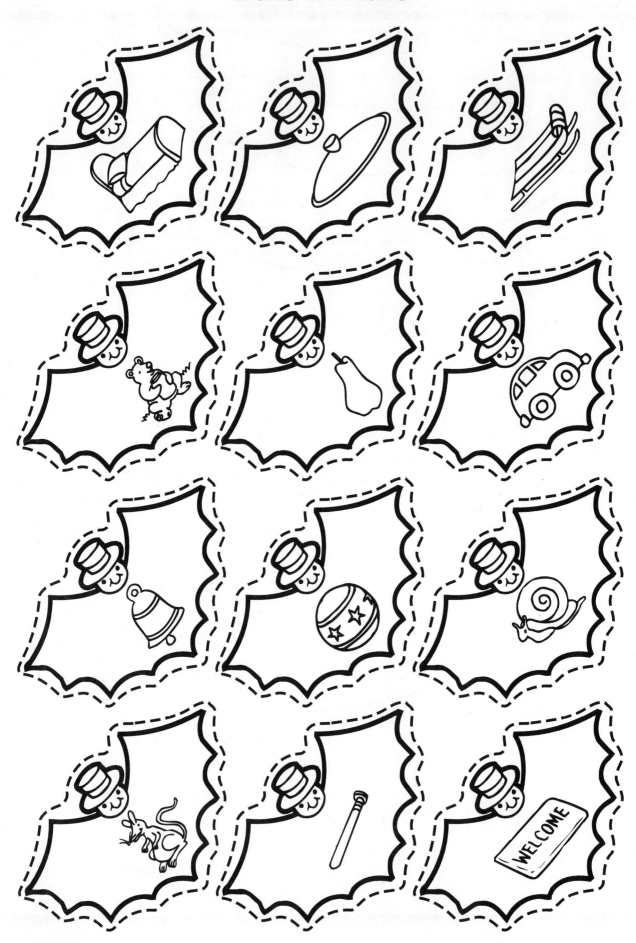

17

Caterpillar

Caterpillar

Final r, b, d, f, g, l, m, n, p, s, t, x

Directions: Two children may play. Take out the picture circles and open the folder. Name the picture on each circle. In turn, take a circle and find the caterpillar section whose picture has the same ending sound. Place all the matching pictures on the caterpillar.

A book to read: <u>The Very Hungry Caterpillar</u> by Eric Carle

Caterpillar

Caterpillar

18. Alligator's Party

Alligator's Party

Short vowels a, i, o

Directions: Take out the T-shirts and open the folder. Name the picture on each T-shirt. Find the animal with the same vowel sound as each picture. Put the T-shirts on the animals.

A book to read: <u>Zack's Alligator</u> by James Watts

DANCE TONIGHT

Alligator's Party

80

19

Ducks in the Pond

Ducks in the Pond

Short vowels u, e

Directions: Take out the ducks and open the folder. Name the picture on each duck. Find the pond with the same vowel sound as each picture. Put the ducks on the matching pond.

A book to read: <u>One Duck, Another Duck</u> by Charlotte Pomerante

Ducks in the Pond

u

Ducks in the Pond

e

Ducks in the Pond

84

The Beetle Band

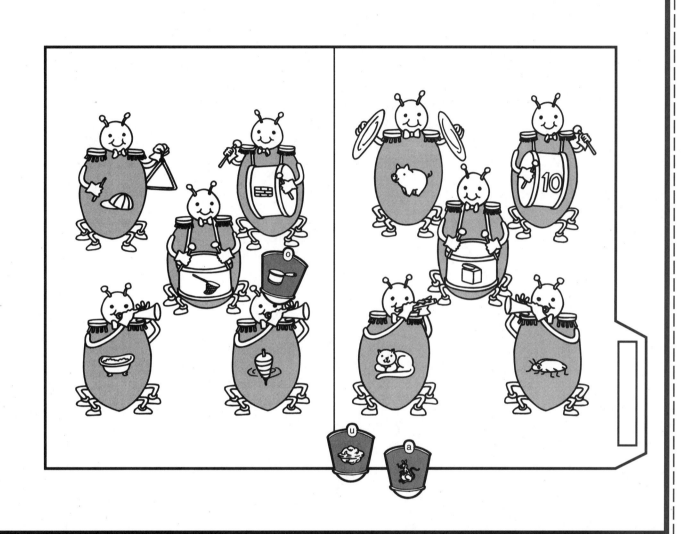

The Beetle Band

All short vowels

Directions: Take out the band hats and open the folder. Name the picture on each hat. Find the beetle whose picture has the same vowel sound. Put the hats on the beetles.

A book to read: Billy's Beetle by Mick Inkpen

The Beetle Band

The Beetle Band

The Beetle Band

Piggy's Ice Cream Sodas

Rhyming picture match

Directions: Take out the ice cream scoops and open the folder. Name the picture on each scoop. Find the soda whose picture rhymes with the picture on each scoop. Put the scoops on the sodas.

A book to read: <u>Pigs Aplenty, Pigs Galore</u> by David McPhail

Piggy's Ice Cream Sodas

Piggy's Ice Cream Sodas

Piggy's Ice Cream Sodas

22. | Mouse Party

Mouse Party

Initial p, c, f, z, t, y, j

Directions: Take out the cheese pieces and open the folder. Name the picture on each piece of cheese. Find the plate whose letter matches the first sound of each picture. Put the cheeses on the plates.

A book to read: Oscar Mouse Finds a Home
by Moira Miller and Maria Majewskai

Mouse Party

Mouse Party

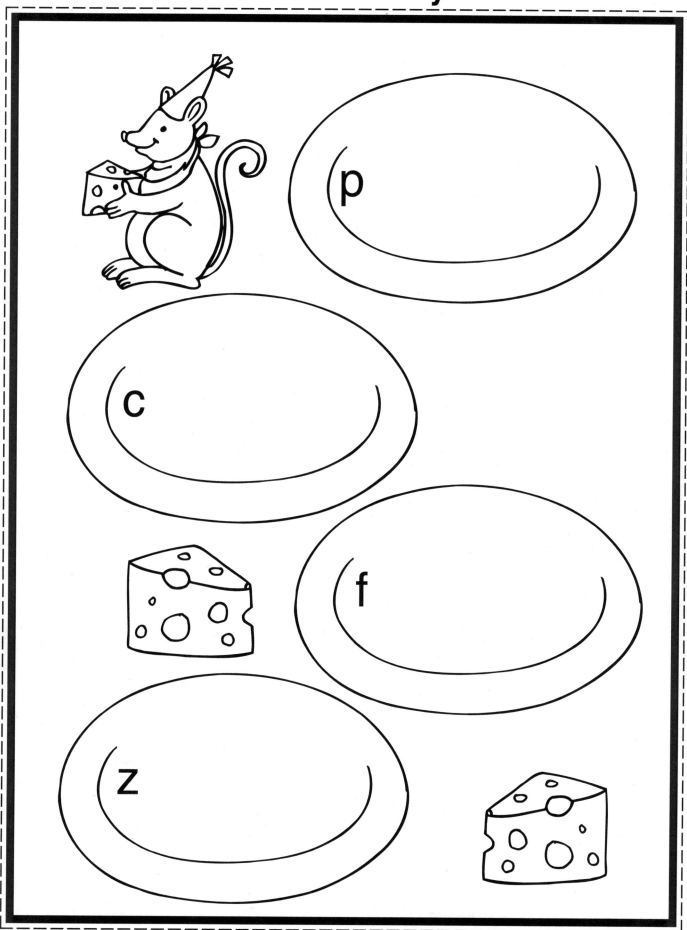

95

Mouse Party

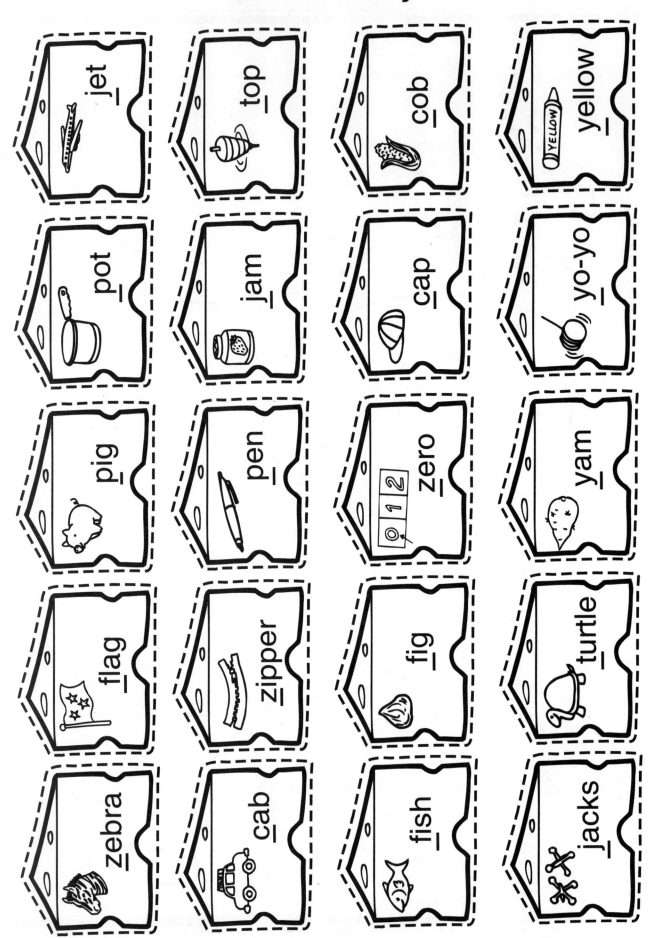

jet

top

cob

yellow

pot

jam

cap

yo-yo

pig

pen

zero

yam

flag

zipper

fig

turtle

zebra

cab

fish

jacks

96

23.

Net the Fish!

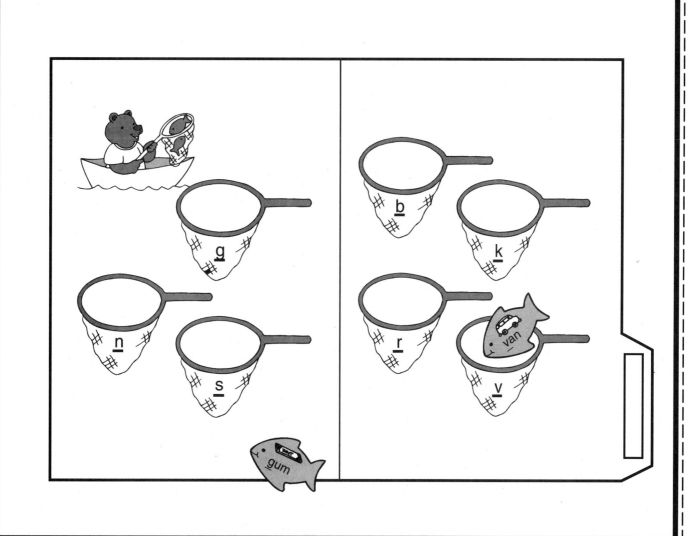

Net the Fish!

Initial g, n, s, k, r, b, v

Directions: Take out the fish and open the folder. Name the picture on each fish. Find the net whose letter matches the first sound of each picture. Put the fish on the nets.

A book to read: <u>Something's Fishy</u> by John Schindal

Net the Fish!

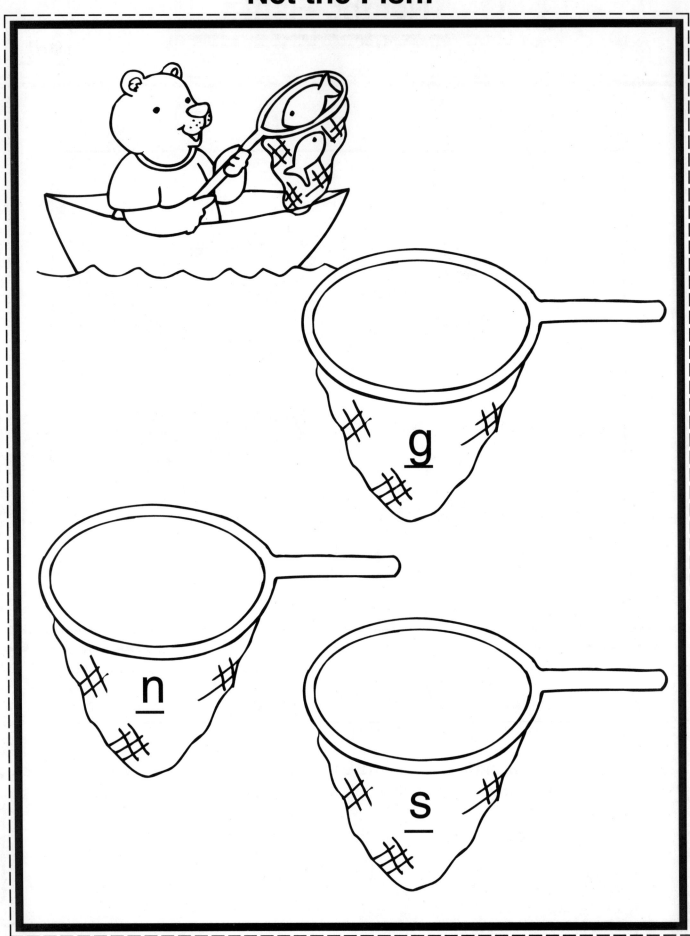

Net the Fish!

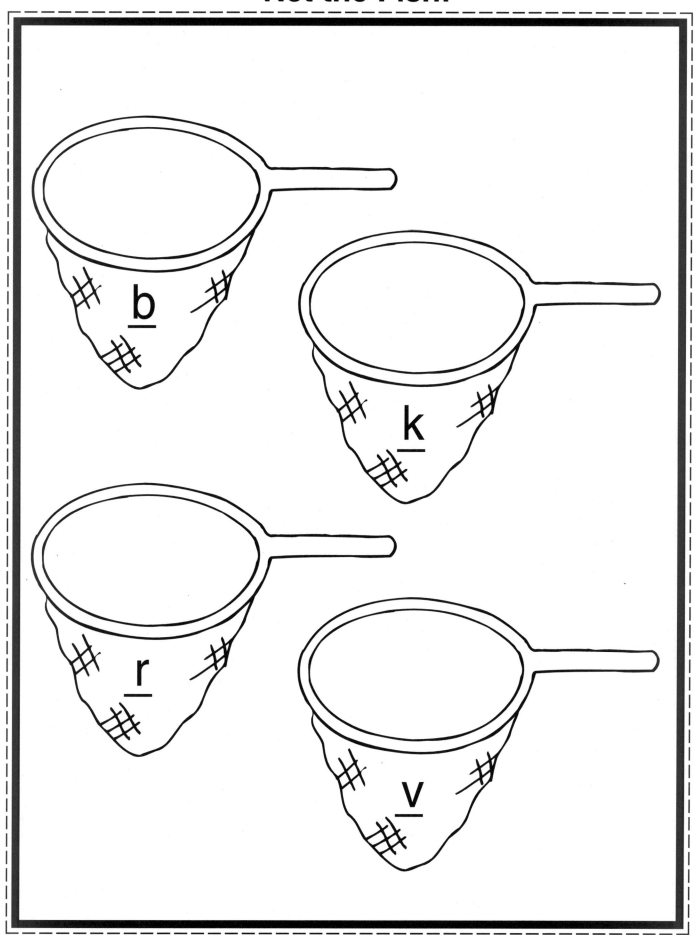

Net the Fish!

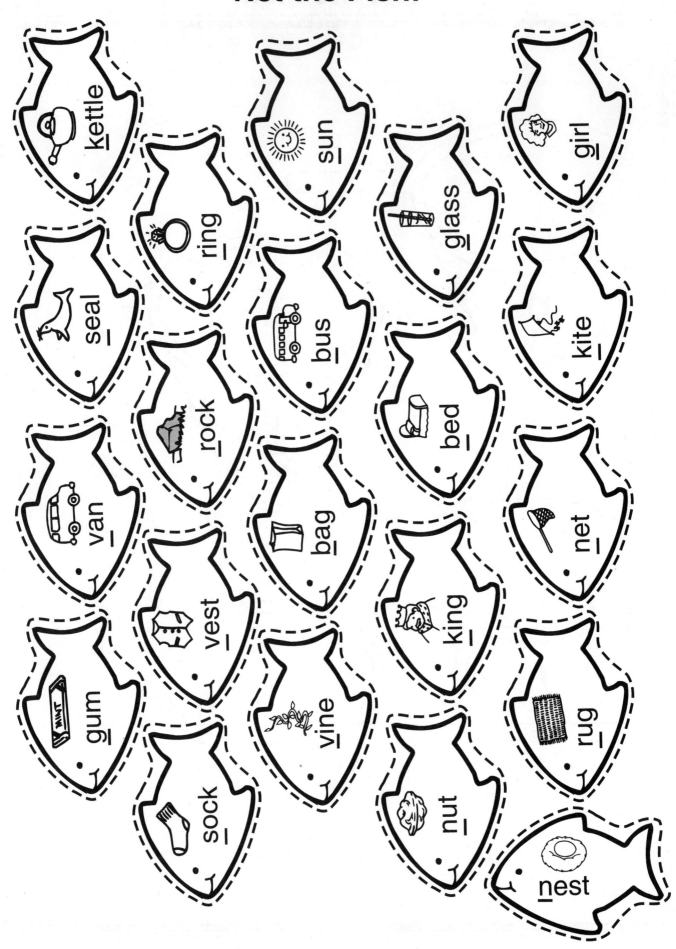

kettle

sun

girl

ring

glass

seal

bus

kite

rock

bed

van

net

bag

vest

king

gum

vine

rug

sock

nut

nest

24. Ants on a Hill

Ants on a Hill

Initial q, l, h, d, m, w

Directions: Take out the picture circles and open the folder. Name the picture on each circle. Find the wheelbarrow whose letter matches the first sound of each picture. Put the circles in the wheelbarrows.

A book to read: Step by Step by Diane Wolkstein

101

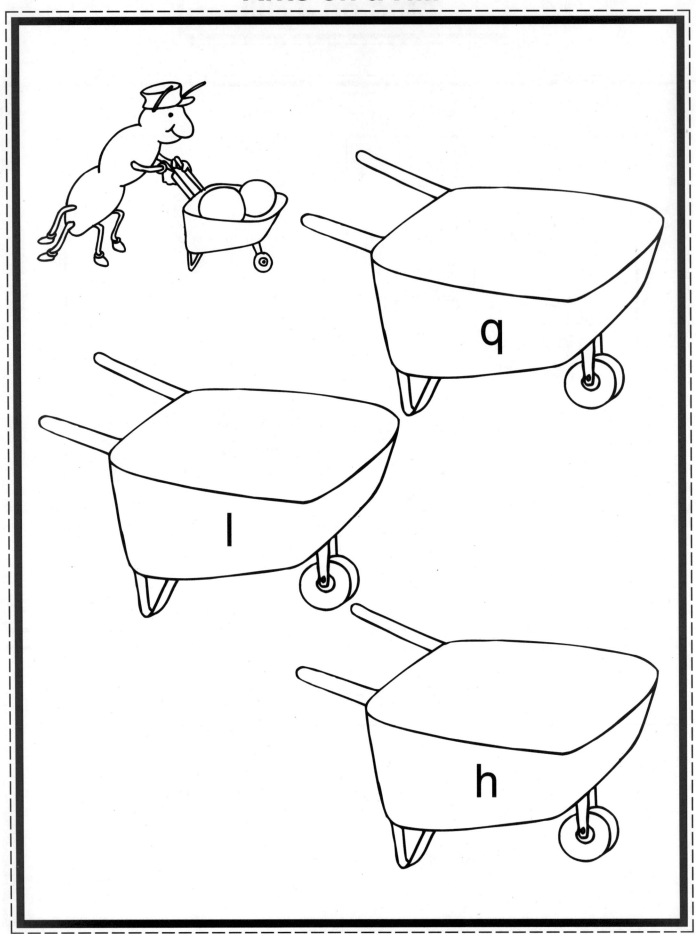

Ants on a Hill

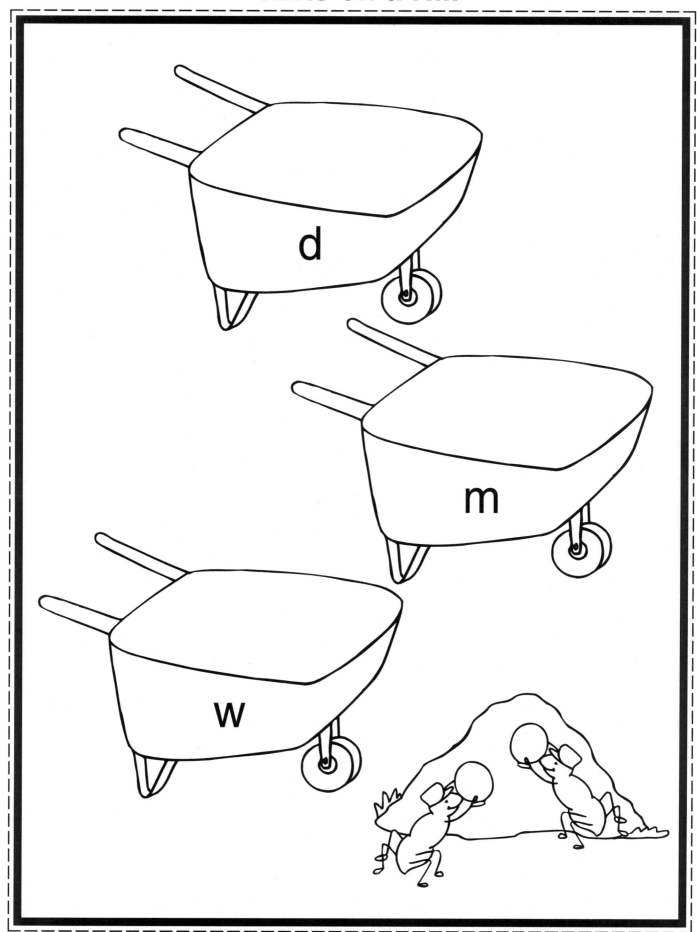

Ants on a Hill

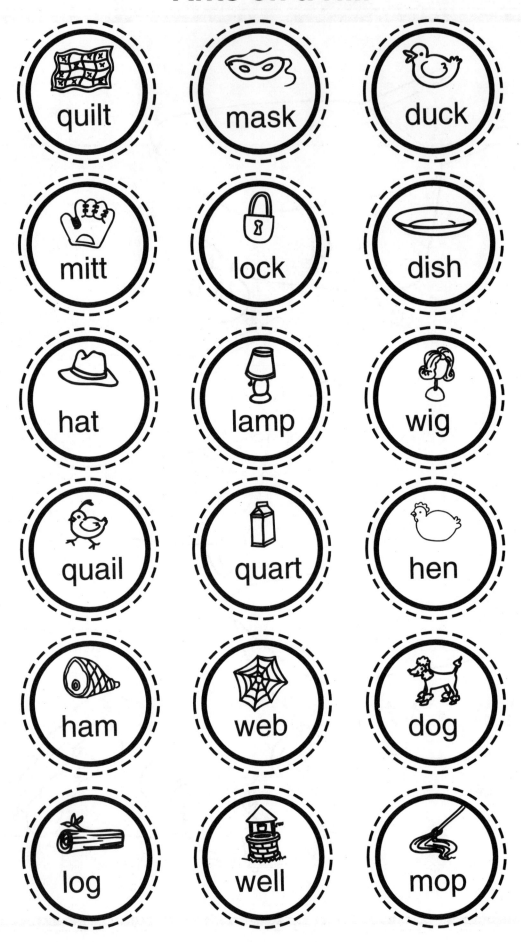

quilt

mask

duck

mitt

lock

dish

hat

lamp

wig

quail

quart

hen

ham

web

dog

log

well

mop

25. Foxes in Boxes

Foxes in Boxes

Final b, f, m, r, t, x

Directions: Take out the foxes and open the folder. Name the picture on each fox. Find the box whose letter matches the first sound of the picture on each fox. Put the foxes in the boxes.

A book to read: <u>Hattie and the Fox</u> by Mem Fox

Foxes in Boxes

_____ b

_____ x

_____ f

Foxes in Boxes

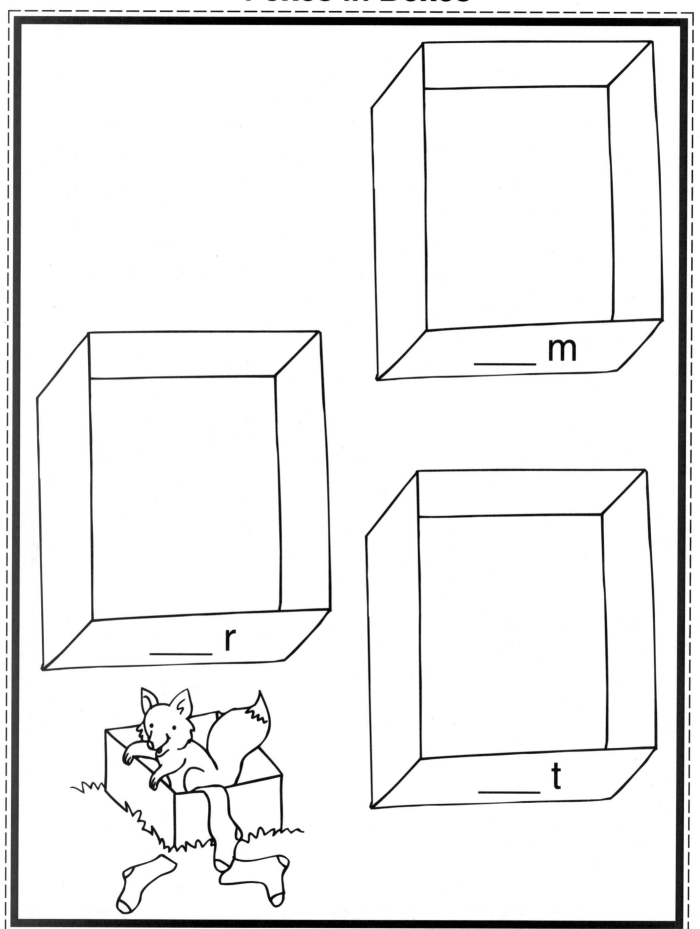

_____ m

_____ r

_____ t

Foxes in Boxes

Bus Station

Final d, g, l, n, p, s

Directions: Take out the window squares and open the folder. Name the picture on each square. Find the bus whose letter matches the last sound of each picture. Put the windows on the buses.

A book to read: <u>The Magic School Bus</u> by Joanna Cole

Bus Station

110

Bus Station

_ d

_ n

_ p

Bus Station

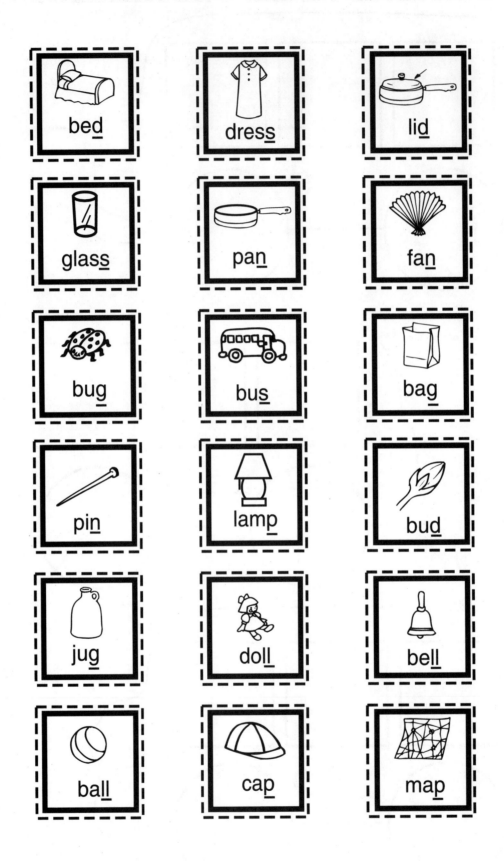

bed

dress

li<u>d</u>

glas<u>s</u>

pa<u>n</u>

fa<u>n</u>

bug

bu<u>s</u>

bag

pi<u>n</u>

lam<u>p</u>

bu<u>d</u>

jug

dol<u>l</u>

bel<u>l</u>

bal<u>l</u>

ca<u>p</u>

ma<u>p</u>

27

Otters and Shells

Otters and Shells

Initial a, e, i, o, u

Directions: Take out the shells and open the folder. Name the picture on each shell. Find the otter whose vowel sound is the same as each picture. Put the shells on the otters.

A book to read: Otters Under Water by Jim Arnosky

Otters and Shells

Otters and Shells

Otters and Shells

apple

ant

alligator

ax

elephant

elf

envelope

egg

igloo

ink

Indian

inch

umbrella

up

inch

under

octopus

umpire

ostrich

olives

ox

28

Frogs on a Log

Frogs on a Log

Medial a, e, i, o, u

Directions: Take out the frogs and open the folder. Name the picture on each frog. Find the log with the same vowel sound as each picture. Put the frogs on the logs.

A book to read: <u>Hop Jump</u> by Ellen Stroll

Frogs on a Log

118

Frogs on a Log

Frogs on a Log

c_at

h_and

cr_ab

w_eb

n_est

j_et

w_ig

sh_ip

p_in

l_og

m_op

b_ox

s_un

b_ug

n_ut

Dinosaur Rhymes

Rhyming word families

Directions: Take out the little dinosaurs and open the folder. Name the picture on each little dinosaur. Find the big dinosaur that has the same rhyme ending as each picture. Put the little dinosaurs on the big dinosaurs.

A book to read: The Day of the Dinosaur by Stan and Jan Berenstain

Dinosaur Rhymes

at

ub

in

Dinosaur Rhymes

123

Dinosaur Rhymes

f a n

p a n

c a n

j u g

m u g

r u g

b i b

c r i b

r i b

c a t

h a t

b a t

c u b

t u b

s u b

f i n

p i n

t w i n

30. | Color Wagon

Color Wagon

Color words

Directions: Two children may play. Take out the spinner and the markers. Open the folder. In turn, spin the spinner and read the color word where the spinner stops. Find the color word on a wagon and put a marker on it. See who can find and read all the color words on his or her wagon first.

A book to read: Carousel by Pat Cummings

Color Wagon

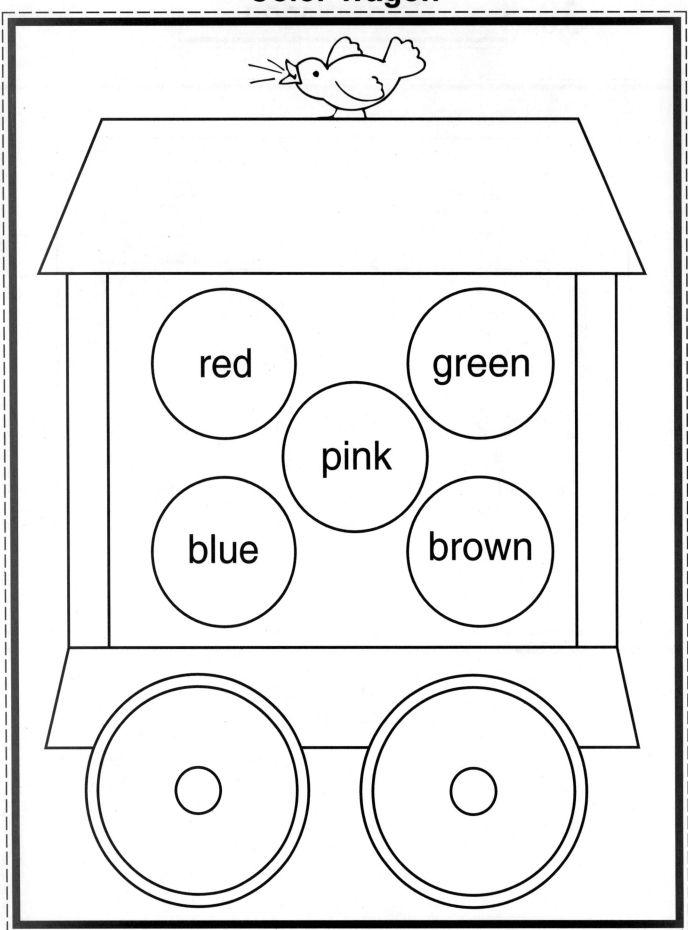

Color Wagon

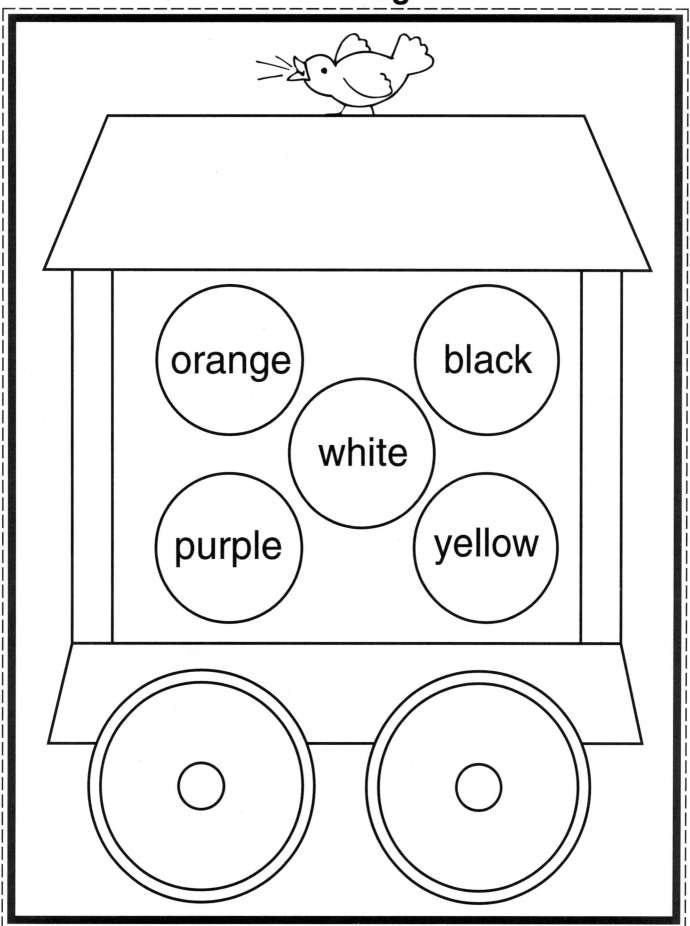

127

Color Wagon

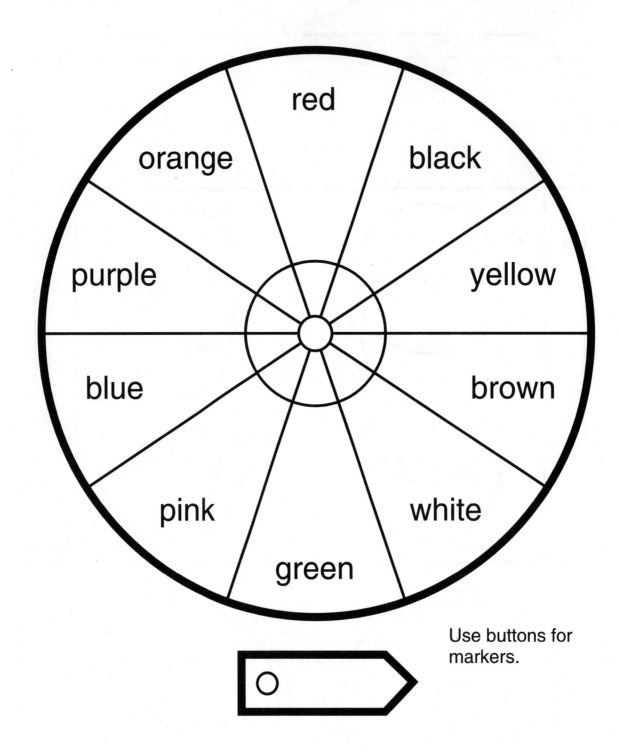

red

black

orange

yellow

purple

blue

brown

pink

white

green

Use buttons for markers.

128

31

Merry-go-round

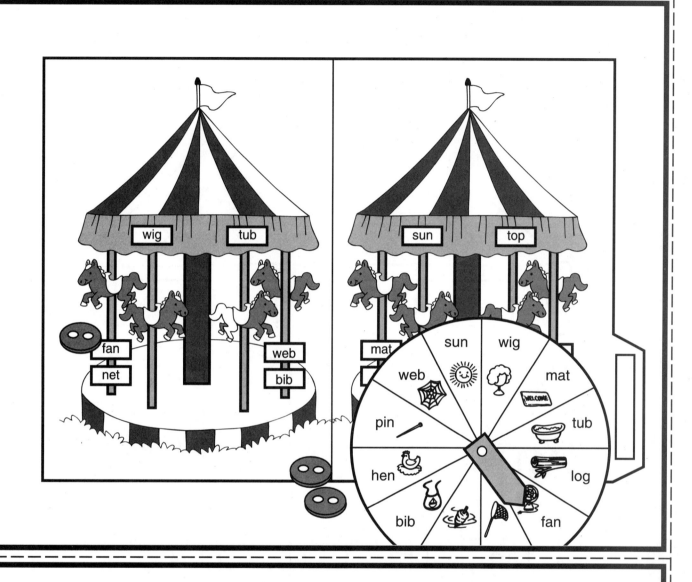

Merry-go-round

Reading short vowel words

Directions: Two children may play. Take out the spinner and the markers. Open the folder. In turn, spin the spinner and read the word where the spinner stops. Find the word on a merry-go-round. Put a marker on the word. See who can find and read all the words on his or her merry-go-round first.

A book to read: <u>The Color Box</u> by Dayle Ann Dodds

Merry-go-round

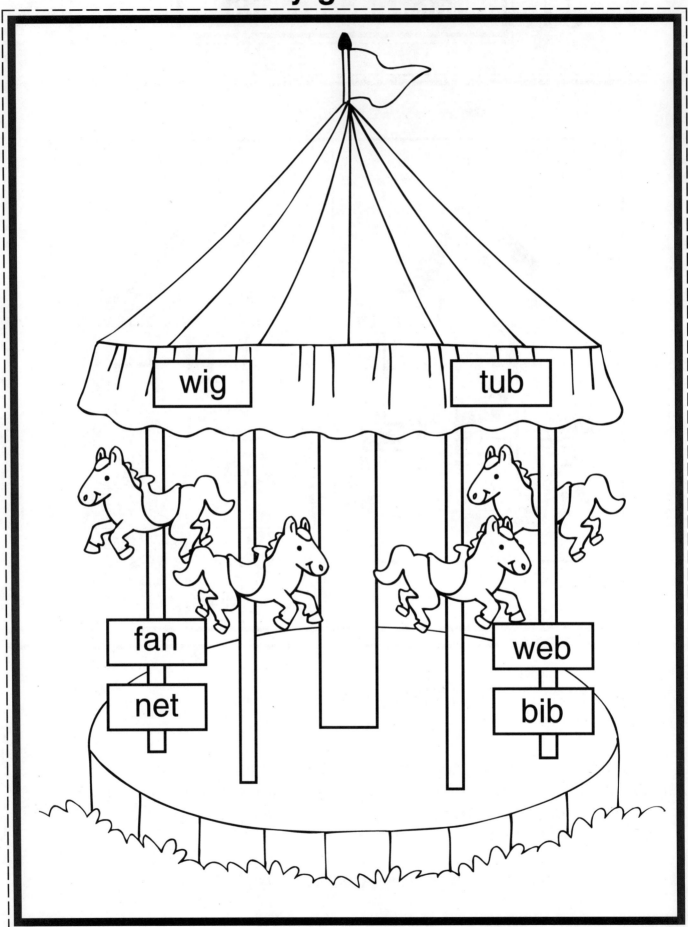

wig

tub

fan

net

web

bib

Merry-go-round

131

Merry-go-round

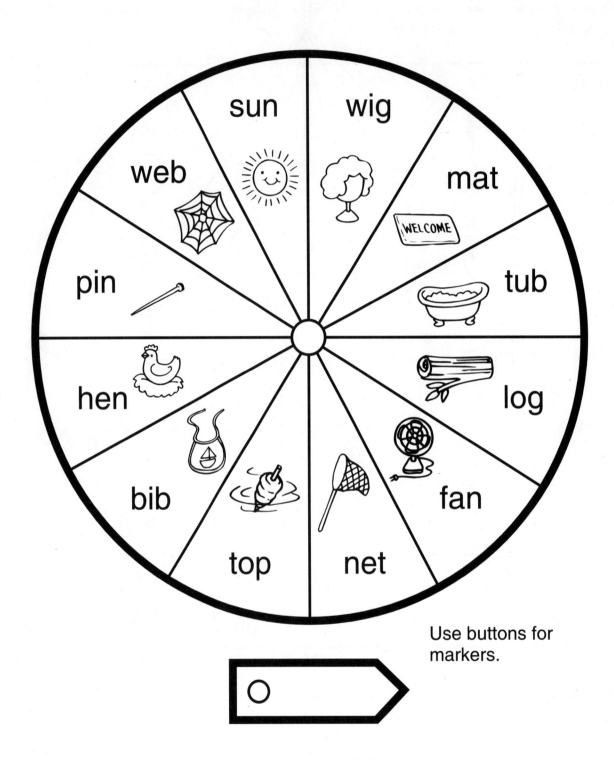

Use buttons for markers.

32

Number Wheel

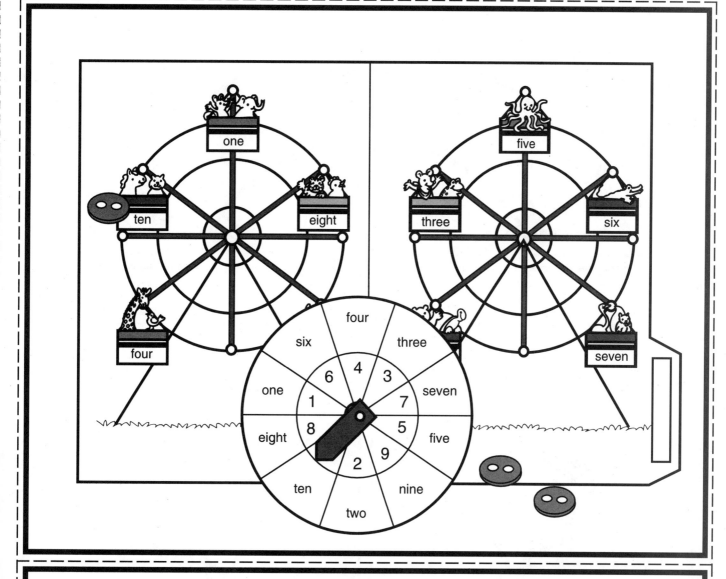

Number Wheel

Number words, one to ten

Directions: Two children may play. Take out the spinner and the markers. Open the folder. In turn, spin the wheel and read the number word where the spinner stops. Find the word on a wheel. Put a marker on the word. See who can find and read all the words on his or her number wheel first.

A book to read: <u>Wheel Away</u> by Dayle Ann Dodds

Number Wheel

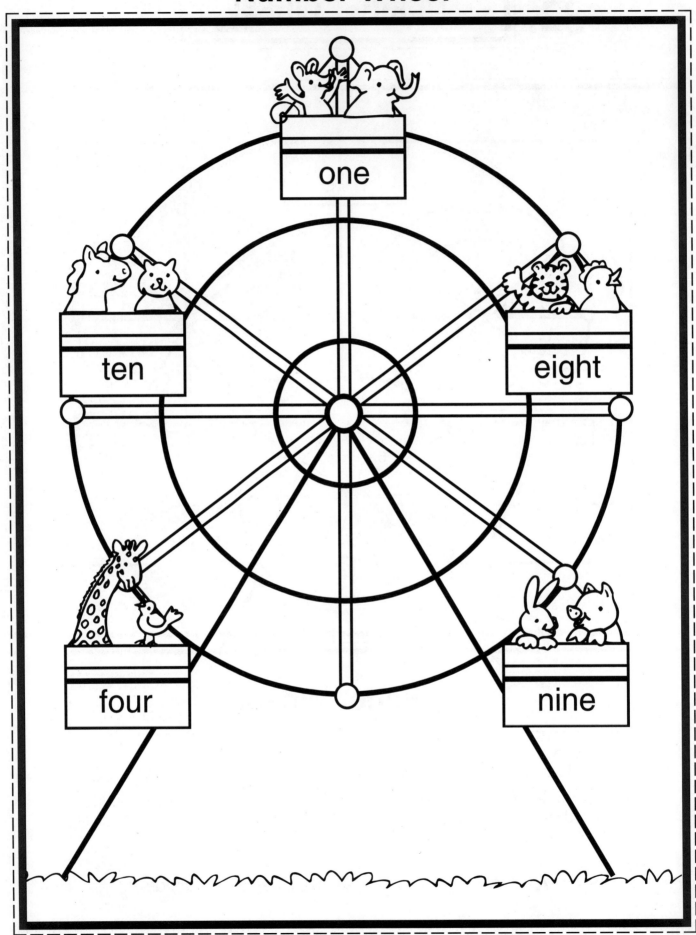

134

Number Wheel

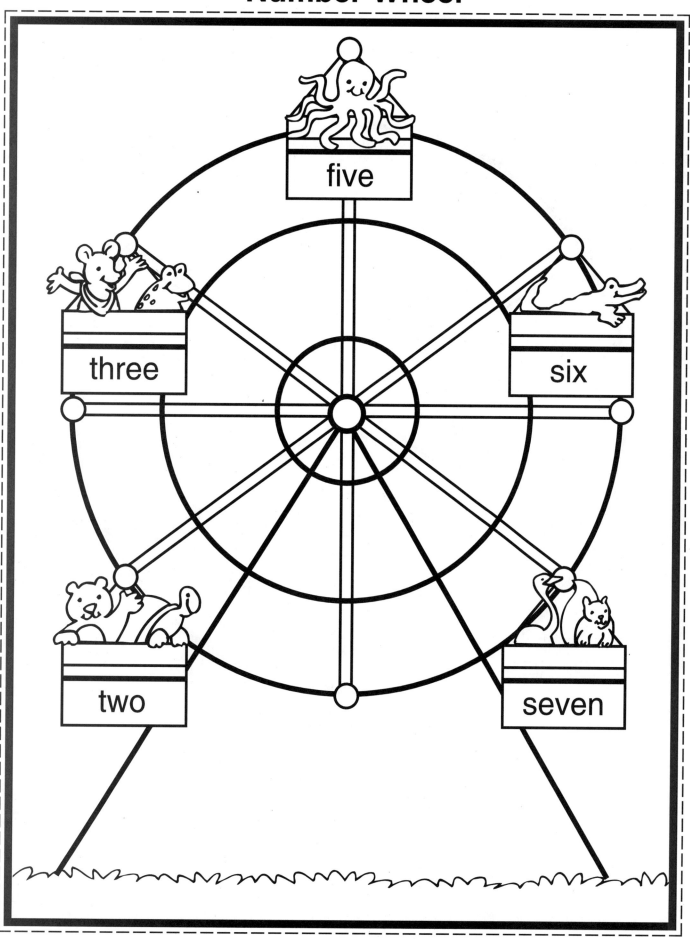

five

three

six

two

seven

Number Wheel

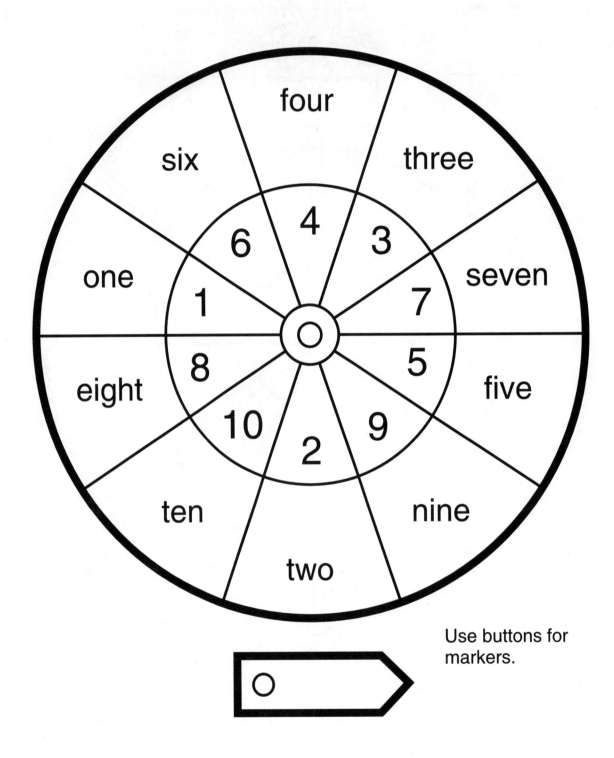

Use buttons for markers.

33. Sight Word Dive

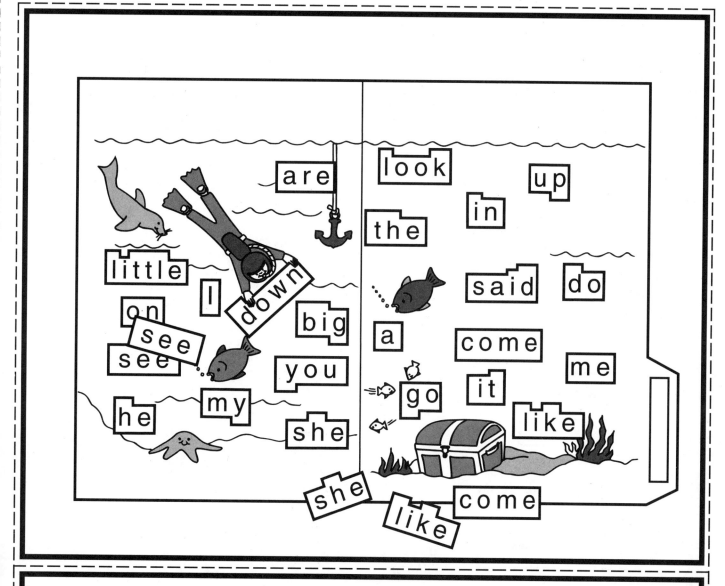

Sight Word Dive

Beginning sight words

Directions: Take out the words and open the folder. Read the words. Find the words that match on the folder. Put each word on the matching word. The shape will help you make the matches.

A book to read: <u>Allistair Underwater</u> by Marilyn Sadler

© 1995 Monday Morning Books, Inc.

137

Sight Word Dive

are

little

I

down

on

big

see

you

he

my

she

Sight Word Dive

look big down

little are up I

like am go a

come the do it

you on he

said in she

see me my

34. | Make a Rainbow

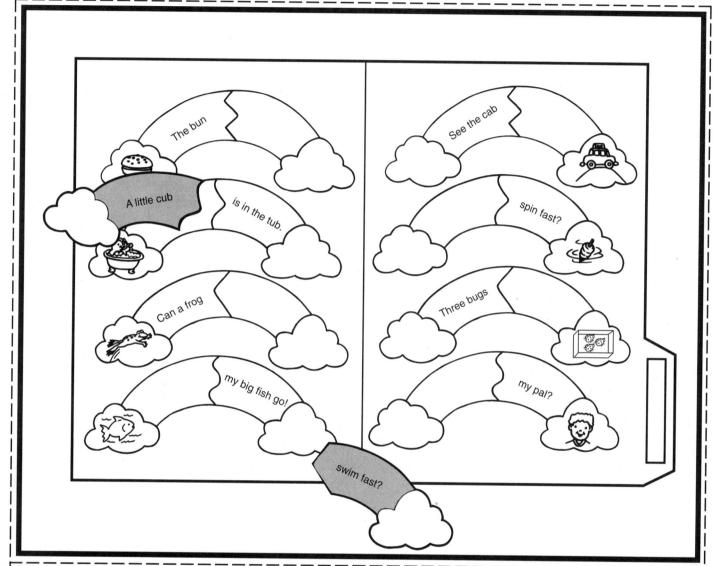

Make a Rainbow

Phrase reading and sentences

Directions: Take out the rainbow parts and open the folder. Read the parts. Place each part on the matching rainbow part on the folder. Read the complete sentence.

A book to read: Planting a Rainbow by Lois Ehlert

Make a Rainbow

The bun

is in the tub.

Can a frog

my big fish go!

Make a Rainbow

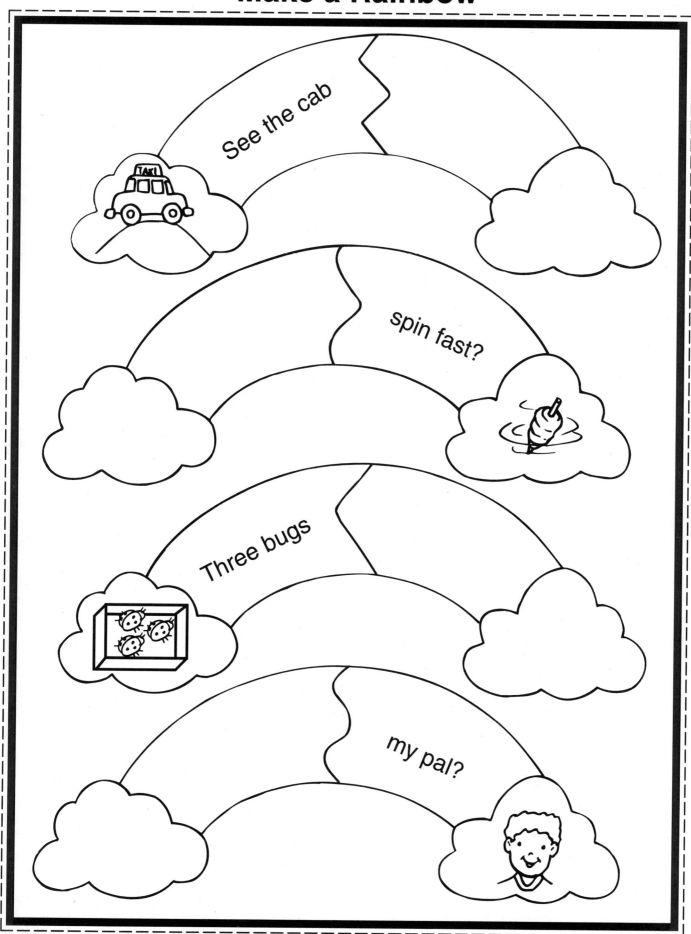

See the cab

spin fast?

Three bugs

my pal?

Make a Rainbow

A little cub

is on the dish.

Can a top

on the hill.

Look at

swim fast?

Are you

sat in the box.

144